The World Has Changed
Coming of Age Stories

Charles A. Bookman

ScanHouse America • Seattle

First published in the United States in 2024 by

ScanHouse America
Visit us at www.scanhouse.us

Copyright © 2024 by Charles A. Bookman

All rights reserved. No part of this book may be reproduced in any form or by any means, electronic or mechanical, without prior permission in writing from the publisher.

ISBN 979-8-218-45701-3 (Softcover)

Printed in the United States of America

Grateful acknowledgment is made for the use of the following: Stray Along the Way; Johnathan Ampersand Esper; Henry Chezar; www.freepik.com; www.drakensberghikes.com

Contents

1. Introduction 6
2. Sail Training 1962—1964 8
3. Introduction to Science 1965 16
4. Young Men and Mountains 1965—1970 21
5. Way Out West 1967 33
6. Political Awakening 1968 48
7. Summer of Love 1968 54
8. Taxi Driver 1968—1970 70
9. Whitehall Street 1969—1970 77
10. Plate Tectonics 1970—1973 81
11. Footloose in South and East Africa 1970 126
12. Hitchhiking Across South America 1971 147
13. Driving the Pan American Highway 1972 153
14. More Roots and Branches 179
15. Coda 201
About the Author 203

"The child is father to the man"

William Wordsworth

Chapter 1

Introduction

Nothing makes you feel old—or young—again like having adolescent grandchildren. Old because you see how different their world is from the one you knew at their age. Remember when phones hung on the wall? When every town had at least one homegrown diner with a great breakfast? When a get-together with friends involved face-to-face communications? When retail shopping required visiting a brick and mortar store? And clubs and social activities were how you met people and picked up gossip. Young because relationships across the ages counter the natural sorting that occurs as we hang out with our own kind. We played bar trivia online during the 2020-2022 pandemic with our daughter-in-law and her friends. Because our team spanned generations, we consistently came out in the top three of twenty teams. For music trivia, our thirteen year old granddaughter joined. She helped every time. Finding a venue to mix with others of different ages and backgrounds—dare I use the word diversity?—this to me is how to keep it fresh. That's

Coming of Age Stories

why I try hard to see the world through our grandchildren's eyes.

As I watch our grandchildren, I am reminded that there is a decade in every life when you spread your wings. The seeds planted in childhood take root. They push up the stalks of the adult you will become. My childhood seeds took root in the decade that spanned the 1960s and 1970s as I explored oceans, mountains and the frontiers of knowledge. I relished the adventure of being on my own. Along the way, I made great friends.

I liked nothing better than exploring somewhere or something new and finding my place in that new world: summers as a teenager on sail training vessels; working in a laboratory at Woods Hole, Massachusetts; building trails for the Forest Service in New Mexico; a roving summer that began in Boise, Idaho, passed through Monterey, California and ended in an epic journey from Wyoming to New York via Little Rock, Arkansas; working on oceanographic ships where strangers became boon companions as we contributed materially to understanding our planet; hitchhiking through the United States and across South America. For a decade, I voyaged into terra incognita searching for myself. Some journeys were more successful than others. All the experiences contributed in some way to the person I became.

My parents, both reporters, encouraged me to record my adventures by writing letters and expecting me to write back. My personal correspondence extends back sixty years. The detail recorded in notes, letters and journals is astounding. The wealth of material makes memoir writing much easier.

And so, I offer this account to my grandchildren and to others who may find something of value in my coming-of-age journey. I wonder, in making this offering, whether the world has changed so much that my youthful exploits might no longer be possible in the twenty-first century's overinformed, overordered world. Do young people still hitchhike across continents? Do they still follow their curiosity to "blank spaces" on the map just to see what's there? And when they get there, are they offered a seat on the fender of a tractor? Or, has the tourism already been organized for them?

Chapter 2

Sail Training 1962—1964

How did I end up spending my adolescent summers on sail training vessels? I sailed as often as I could at summer camp, and when camp was in the rear view mirror my mother asked around and learned about "Captain" Anthony Keasbey, who taught at the Fieldston School, in Bronx, New York, and was a lieutenant in the Canadian naval reserve. Keasbey owned and operated a small sail training schooner, *Harelda*, along Nova Scotia's fogbound coast. *Harelda* looked exactly like Canada's famous schooner *Bluenose*, which won the International Fisherman's Cup Race off Halifax, Nova Scotia in 1921 and which appears on the Canadian dime. But at 58 feet, *Harelda* was a good deal smaller. Keasbey (his crew called him "Skipper") happily welcomed me to his thirteen member teenage crew in the summer of 1962, and I returned to *Harelda* in 1964 to participate in the first global gathering of tall ships known as Operation Sail.

Coming of Age Stories

Nova Scotia, 1962

It's a little hard for me to believe now, especially as a grandparent of teenagers, but when I was all of fourteen years old, my parents put me on a propeller plane to Halifax, Nova Scotia, Canada. Faced with a six hour layover in Boston, I found a cab driver to show me the city's historic sights: Faneuil Hall, North Church, and the Commons. My plane arrived in Halifax too late for me to travel down coast to meet *Harelda* at Mahone Bay, so I checked into a motel. The next morning, I took a cab to the bus station and rode two hours to Mahone Bay. There was a fish and chips shop at the village pier, where I ordered lunch and munched contentedly while waiting for my ship to come in.

If I suggested to my daughter-in-law that she send her teenager to another country with only the vaguest idea of how to get to their destination, to stay unaccompanied in a motel, find their way to the bus station, and then ride down an unfamiliar coast and debark at an isolated pier, she would tell me where to go— and it wouldn't be Canada!

I recorded my summer's adventures on *Harelda* in my journal, including an afternoon in the historic fishing port of Lunenberg. There, I chatted with an old man sitting on a keg on the fishing dock. He introduced himself as Captain Henry Larsen, the first man to navigate through the Northwest Passage. Captain Larsen was a bona fide Canadian hero. Today, his patrol ship, the *St. Roch*, is the centerpiece of Vancouver's Maritime Museum. Touring that ship a few years ago brought back memories of my own great adventure.

Harelda was primitive. We slept in narrow open bunks along the sides of the common area below deck. The engine was a marine conversion of an old Ford Model A that required a hand crank to start. There was no refrigerator, and we cooked on a wood stove. For navigation, we relied on an AM radio with a directional antenna. Back then, radio towers were shown on the nautical charts, so if you tuned into a station and then adjusted the antenna for maximum and minimum reception, you could

Charles A. Bookman | **The World Has Changed**

chart a bearing to that station's transmitter. Do that for two different AM stations, and where the bearing lines crossed was your approximate position.

This method of navigation was helpful but it led to an occasional hair raising encounter. One occurred on the heels of a squall near the Sambro Shoals, outside of Halifax. In a letter, I wrote about a very challenging watch:

> At about 3:30 a.m. we were awakened by the beginning of a real August gale with driving rain, biting cold, and 15-foot waves. It was my turn at the wheel. I tried to keep *Harelda* from catching the waves broadside and swamping; the wind was too high to come about, a turning maneuver that we had to make or we would end up on a sandbar. Wearing a lifeline, Skipper backed the jib amidst huge waves. That brought the bow around, but *Harelda* was under extreme strain. Our three-rope hold on the rowboat snapped. Three ropes! Imagine that! There went a hundred dollar dinghy, lost forever in the storm.
>
> I felt lonely and a little frightened, on deck, at the helm, with no dinghy at 5 a.m. in a gale. All of a sudden, I panicked! Frightened, I yelled for Skipper! The stays (metal wires that support the mast) had parted. The mainmast was swaying, about to snap. And me at the wheel.
>
> Down below, things were a mess. The lower end of the mainmast was jumping around, menacing the crew. We tried to lower the mainsail but it fouled in the top springstay. Now the flimsy topmast supported the whole sail. Skipper and I rigged an emergency backstay from the staysail halyard. As day broke, we passed through the Sambro Ledges, a deadly reef just outside Halifax that had sunk many a ship. We figured that with such big waves any water that didn't break would be deep enough for us.
>
> Suddenly, skipper yelled to me to clear the cauly float (a type of raft), then he gave me the helm. He had noticed that to our left lay a rocky, dangerous lee shore, and dead ahead lay the little "Isle of Mann." A rockpile loomed halfway between them. *Harelda*, under drastically reduced sail area, was drifting sideways faster than she was moving forward. Lastly, her primitive Model A-era marine engine was wet and flooded. In case we had to abandon ship, I tried to bring the ship around while at the same time arousing the crew be-

Coming of Age Stories

low deck. Skipper worked at the bow, preparing three anchors that he heaved overboard just in time to keep *Harelda* off the rocks.

It was daytime now, and luckily a passing fisherman towed us into port. After we secured *Harelda* to the wharf—just as nicely as you please, Skipper came up to me and said, "I couldn't have done it without you."

Months later, Skipper wrote a letter of reference that helped me secure a berth on the *Provident*. I have a copy of that correspondence too. He wrote:

> This is to recommend Chip Bookman for a berth in your crew. He sailed in mine July and August 1962, proving himself one of its most valuable members. Boarding with some knowledge of sailing, he developed a particular ability for handling the fifty-eight foot schooner both in sailing her at the helm and in all phases of handling sails. His seamanship was also of the kind that can be depended upon at all times, and many details were left to him. He is the type that does what has to be done without being told to but never becomes a meddler in jobs not his.
>
> Once in a storm the skipper had to go forward to tack and back the jumbo (the mate was ashore and the students are not allowed to work the foredeck in dangerous seas) so Chip was chosen to take the wheel and tack the vessel, a very difficult responsibility because of the heavy seas stopping the headway and the windage keeping the vessel from going around. This he accomplished calmly and successfully without wavering.
>
> Later in the same gale it was necessary to lower the mainsail downwind and bring it in over the rail, as it was far too rough to round up and take it down flapping. (We do not use quarter tackles and the boom is long and heavy.) Chip took one halyard and another boy the other, easing the big main down handsomely as several of us gathered it in, though he had never seen it done this way before, nor been in such a sea or storm. Then he stood by as port was approached, planning the approach direction, entrance, sail-trimming, and anchoring and executing most of them himself.
>
> Finally, Chip's gentlemanliness, obedience, honour, consideration for ship and shipmates, continued interest in ships and maritime lore, and ability to maintain equilibrium and happy humour

unfalteringly in the narrow confines of a small ship combine to recommend him most urgently for further crew positions, such as in your esteemed ship. May he prove as loyal to you and her as he was to mine!

Captain Keasbey was a prince among men and I am grateful for the experiences I had on his historic vessel.

Provident 1963

With my mother's great success shipping me out with Captain Keasbey in the summer of 1962, while planning a family summer trip to Europe in 1963, she wrote to a dean of British sailing, popular maritime author Alan Villiers. As a young man he had sailed on the last clipper ships to navigate around Cape Horn. Villiers put her in touch with the Island Sailing Club out of Salcombe, Devon, England. The club had recently restored an 80-foot Brixham trawler, the *Provident*, which the club was operating as a sail training vessel.

I joined the historic ketch-rigged *Provident* for two weeks in August 1963. Most of her crew were young adults on summer holiday. I was younger than the others by perhaps a decade but the age difference didn't matter as we were there to learn and were assigned regular watch duties. We sailed to Plymouth, then to the Isle of Guernsey. From Guernsey we called at Saint Malo, France, then crossed the channel back to Salcombe.

Provident was much more comfortable than *Harelda*. She had a well-stocked and staffed galley, the bunks were in small cabins, and the crew gathered in a comfortable midships saloon.

Provident still sails as of this writing (2024). In a video from 2017 on Youtube (https://www.youtube.com/watch?v=FRE-Ht-n5y6U), she's pitching and rolling as she departs the port of Torquay, in Devon. She looks the same and that's about how I remember her (pitching and rolling!).

Coming of Age Stories

Operation Sail 1964

My Operation Sail 1964 program booklet turned up in a moldy box of memorabilia, with its handsome royal blue cover and spiral binding intact. The program contained photos and descriptions of all the vessels that participated in the first weeklong global celebration of tall sailing ships. The tall ships gathered in New York Harbor in July 1964. The celebration included a sail-by past the Statue of Liberty, a ticker tape parade down lower Broadway to City Hall, and celebratory balls at the Chelsea piers (when they were still working finger piers).

Most of the eighteen tall ships that paraded in New York Harbor were sail training vessels. The US Coast Guard's *Eagle* (a war prize formerly known as the *Horst Wessel*) led the parade. The *Libertad* came from Argentina and the *Esmeralda* from Chile. Portugal's *Sagres*, a barque, joined the flotilla along with Spain's four-masted schooner, *Juan Sebastian de Elcano*. Norway and Denmark sent the full-rigged ships *Christian Radich* and *Danmark*.

Canada sent the *Bluenose II*, a replica of the famous fishing and racing schooner whose likeness graces the Canadian dime, and another traditionally designed coastal schooner, *Harelda*. At fifty-eight feet stem to stern, she was among the smallest participants in Operation Sail. Carrying a seasonal crew of thirteen teenage cadets. I was privileged to be among them.

We were a day late to the party and missed the sail-by. Therein lies a tale. It was a dark and stormy night ... actually, it was calm and foggy. The fog trapped us in a small rocky cove on the southern Nova Scotia coast for two days, throwing us off schedule. We crossed the edge of Georges Bank at night with a brisk wind on our quarter. I recall passing large Soviet "fishing trawlers" operating off the mouth of Long Island Sound. The trawlers were there to track submarine activity from the naval base at Groton, Connecticut.

I was at the helm as we approached Long Island Sound a day later than planned. It was night, the moon was in its last quarter

Charles A. Bookman | **The World Has Changed**

Operation Sail 1964 Brochure

and fog hung low over the waves. The others were below deck enjoying cocoa before turning in for the night or until the next watch. Suddenly my thoughts were interrupted. Peering intently ahead through light fog, I could just make out the white line of surf on the shore of Block Island. I hollered for help.

The Author at the Helm Approaching New York Harbor

Coming of Age Stories

We turned the boat around, but not before running up hard on a sand shoal. We hit bottom around 9 p.m., close to low tide. I could hear the surf and see the bluffs of Block Island from where we struck. With two sets of oars in the dory, we pulled *Harelda* off an hour later as the tide came in. Skipper looked below. The hard knock had cracked a board or shaken some oakum loose and we were taking on water. We all took turns pumping out the bilge every hour as we continued our way down Long Island Sound.

I kept the helm as *Harelda* sailed the East River to her berth near 23rd Street. Even as we marched in the ticker tape parade and attended the gala events, we still had to take turns keeping the bilge pumped.

After all the hoopla, Skipper took *Harelda* to a shipyard on City Island, where she was hauled out and her bottom re-caulked. Her sail back to Nova Scotia was uneventful.

My time on *Harelda* was one of the highlights of my adolescence. In the space of thirty-six hours, I had nearly wrecked the ship I loved, and then piloted her triumphantly through the Hell's Gate and down the East River into the city I called home. While we missed the nautical parade, we were still part of a historic celebration of the age of sail.

Operation Sail 1964 initiated a revival of tall ship celebrations. New York Harbor hosted the tall ships again as part of the 1976 Bicentennial. *Harelda* sleeps with the fishes now, but other tall ships still sail the seas. Some, like Norway's steel-hulled *Christian Radich* now operate in the cruise trade. You can find out more about the tall ships at https://tallshipsnetwork.com/voyages/ .

Chapter 3

Introduction to Science 1965

Talent and hard work help you run the race but connections sometimes provide a shortcut to the starting gate. Mindful of the value of an internship on the road to college, a research professor friend of the family recommended me to a colleague who planned to spend the summer studying RNA's relationship to DNA at the Marine Biological Laboratory (MBL) in Woods Hole, Massachusetts. The discovery of the double helix was just a decade old. RNA's role in cell biology was not yet understood, and that summer scientist needed a laboratory assistant to help him run experiments on sea urchin embryos, which would hopefully play a role in that RNA research.

I spent that summer tagging sea urchin embryos with radioactive markers and then tracing the replication of RNA and DNA through four cell division cycles. I ran the experiments for the research scientist. Each experimental run took about sixteen

Coming of Age Stories

hours from start to finish. A typical work day began at 8 a.m. with a trip to the supply shed, where I would pick up a bushel of sea urchins. Returning to the lab, I would zap them with an electric current or inject them with potassium chloride to extract their eggs and sperm. Next, I would mix the material in a beaker and then use a microscope to follow the cell division until we had clusters of thirty-two cells. We concentrated the cells in a centrifuge and then ran them through a machine that measured the concentration of radioactive tracers. The experiment would wrap up about midnight. The next day, I would clean the lab in preparation for doing it all over again.

With my father at the Marine Biological Laboratory

As lab work permitted, I explored Woods Hole. Home to major scientific institutions including the Marine Biological Laboratory, where I worked, Woods Hole Oceanographic Institution, which operated oceanographic ships and even a new diving submersible called *Alvin,* and a US government fisheries laboratory, in summer the town attracted vacationing academics from across the northeast and around the world. A busy drawbridge connected Eel Pond, where the MBL kept its little fleet that every day dredged up more sea urchins for me, with the rest of the port. Car ferries sailed for Martha's Vineyard and Nantucket. Nearby, oceanographic equipment-crammed docks berthed the Woods Hole Oceanographic Institution's deepwater vessels the *Atlantis II* and the *Chain*.

I was still in high school, living with graduate students and sharing our lab with investigators from Chicago and Britain. I was, for the first time, on my own in a community of smart, motivated adults. Down the hall, another high school intern operated an electron microscope. We would occasionally lunch together in the cafeteria or at the nearby pizza place where he sometimes washed dishes. Little did I know that Robert Spindel would become a lifelong friend and that Robert's father, Bill Spindel, who taught chemistry at Columbia University and had worked on the Manhattan Project that developed the atomic bomb, would help connect me a decade later with professional staff at the National Research Council of the National Academy of Sciences, where I would build my career. Robert and I reconnected a year later at Columbia University and we have remained fast friends ever since.

Robert's father Bill eventually became a colleague after I joined the staff of the National Research Council. How that came about is an example of the importance of networking, and of how luck is equal parts preparation and opportunity. I bonded with Robert because we were the youngest interns at MBL in the summer of 1965. Through Robert, I met his father Bill. After an academic career at Columbia University, Bill became director of the Chemistry Advisory Board at the National Research Council. While studying at Einstein College of Medicine in New York City, Robert would visit me occasionally when I worked for the Maryland Coastal Zone Management Program and lived south of Annapolis. He often brought his father along. On one of Bill's visits with his son Robert, I discussed my interest in science and shared that I was looking for professional opportunities in Washington, DC. The next time Bill visited, he gave me a copy of the National Research Council's Annual Report. Running to hundreds of pages, the volume listed every board and committee, their members and professional staff. Thumbing through

Coming of Age Stories

the volume, I noted boards that advised government agencies on maritime activities, marine engineering, oceanography, and the environment, all subjects that interested me and in which I believed I had some relevant academic and professional background. Using the annual report, I made cold calls to several professional staff. The director of the Maritime Transportation Research Board, which worked primarily for the federal Maritime Administration and US Coast Guard, invited me to visit. I spent an enjoyable, informative afternoon with policy experts who managed advisory boards and projects on ships and shipping. One of them, Harvey Paige, shared a carpool with another staff officer, Donald Perkins, who had just joined another board, the Marine Board. Don mentioned to Harvey that he had been tasked with organizing a workshop on ocean engineering in the Arctic and he needed an editor to help him with the proceedings. Harvey mentioned my visit that afternoon, Don took note and after a telephone interview and a brief meeting with Don's boss, the Marine Board director, retired Navy captain Jack W. Boller, I began working as an editorial consultant for the Marine Board. That led to a twenty-year career in science policy; I eventually served as director of the Marine Board.

Exhilarated by my summer of science, my college application essay that fall centered on my interest in research. I wrote, "I left Woods Hole with a sense of what research is all about. The methods of research must be learned by experience, and when learned, can be applied to any field of investigation. This summer, I was steeped in research day in and day out, learning constantly how to seek facts, how to discover. The 'bug' to probe and investigate has taken me for life." The seeds that were planted sexing sea urchins in the lab that long-ago summer led more or less directly to my early professional work as a seagoing technician and my first full career in science policy at the National Research Council. The scientists who helped me—the medical researcher who took a chance on a high school kid and the friend's father who took an interest in helping me find professional work in line with my experience and abilities were mentors at critical moments. Their early interest helped me find and land opportunities that launched me into a career in marine and environmental science and engineering policy. Mindful of the cascading effect of their early interest and assistance, I always try to pay it forward by encouraging young people and helping them make connections where I can.

Chapter 4
Young Men and Mountains 1965—1970

Introduction to Winter Mountaineering 1965

I keep a private museum of antique mountaineering gear in my basement. Prominently displayed are vintage wood and gut snowshoes in the shape of beaver tails. True anachronisms when compared to today's sleek, light models, we used these in New Hampshire's White Mountains and New York's Adirondacks in the 1960s. We climbed with external frame backpacks laden with 70 pounds of gear.

Some of that gear remains in my private museum. There is the Optimus 111B gas stove with its strong pump and robust metal case. The stove burned white gas, which we carried in metal canisters. It was powerful enough to melt gallons of snow. Of course the process of melting snow into drinking water produced clouds of steam that turned into frost on the wall of the tent.

Charles A. Bookman | **The World Has Changed**

Eventually in winter camping, the frost ends up in one's clothes and sleeping bag, reducing the insulation value and adding to the weight you carry.

My down sleeping bag and expedition parka are also in my museum. These remain wonders of needlework with their thick down that, even today, would still keep me warm in a snow cave. The main problem with the old gear is not the down, it's the zippers, which have become brittle.

The author at the start of the Presidential Range Traverse

I wore heavy surplus pants and a wool shirt. My feet were protected by *Mickey Mouse* boots, double-insulated rubber boots originally developed for fighter pilots in the Korean War. Over the boots, we pulled on large nylon *Mukluks*, an overboot that ran up to the knee. Somehow, the footwear fit into the snowshoes. For wind protection, I favored a *cagoule*, a cross between an anorak (parka) and a poncho. The garment went over everything and hung down to the knees. Our double-thickness gloves were also Korean war surplus, like the boots. Some even had trigger fingers. We affixed them with long straps that wound behind our necks so that they wouldn't blow away if we had to take them off in the wind.

My first winter mountaineering adventure was organized by a high school teacher who had climbed Mount Washington, the

Coming of Age Stories

highest peak in New England, with the Dartmouth Outing Club. A dozen of us lumbered in our old school bus up to Pinkham Notch, New Hampshire, where the Appalachian Mountain Club still maintains an outing center. Up and at 'em before dawn, we snowshoed a couple of miles over to the carriage road, a long looping dirt track that leads up to a complex of buildings—a weather station, TV antennas, and housing for the people who maintain and monitor them. I didn't know it then, but I would walk the carriage road many times over the next few years as it is the safest winter route up Mount Washington and into the Presidential Range. The carriage road is open in summer to tourists and is used in winter by Sno-Cats, which supply the complex at the summit.

Even though the carriage road is safer than other routes, it is hardly a cakewalk. Snowshoes will carry you up to the halfway point. Beyond that, high winds compact the snow and crampons become necessary. Above timberline, strong winds try to push you off the road into the Great Gulf. For the safety of the Sno-Cat operators, small and stout wooden emergency sheds had been constructed and chained down along the upper reaches. With two companions, I once sheltered for two nights and a full day in one of these sheds after a winter storm overtook us.

Our high school bunch was long on enthusiasm and short on skill. We turned around an hour short of the summit in order to return to Pinkham Notch before dark. While we hadn't summited, we had used our crampons and ice axes, and everyone felt the rosy glow of accomplishment.

I didn't realize it then, but I was hooked. Winter mountaineering would become the focus of my winter outdoors activities for the next five years. With the Columbia Mountaineering Club during my college years, I would participate and lead expeditions in the White Mountains and the Adirondacks. Later with friends, I continued these trips, pushing the boundaries of what was doable with the equipment at the time. My companions in these expeditions would go on pushing boundaries. One of them, Johnny Waterman, became well known in Alaska before dying alone in a winter solo attempt to climb the East Buttress of Denali. Looking back, I am grateful I still have all of my fingers and toes. We encountered blizzards and wind storms, and endured cold snaps (26 degrees Fahrenheit below zero), and temperature inversions that caused all our gear to go from sopping wet to frozen within hours.

The Adirondack 46ers, 1966

We were young and enthusiastic hikers, but woefully inexperienced. Camping at Giant's Washbowl near the base of one of New York's forty-six named highest Adirondack peaks, the "46ers," we peered intently at the pond's edge as clouds of tiny flies hatched. We didn't know it then, but New York's Adirondack Park empties out every June because of massive swarms of black flies. In addition to their irritating swarming, the flies draw blood and leave itchy red welts as a souvenir. We sheltered in our sleeping bags.

The next day, we climbed Giant Mountain, our first named 46er. With plenty of daylight, we hitchhiked north on Highway 73 to Keene Valley, then walked the Johns Brook Trail, intending to climb the fabled Great Range the following day. Fortunately, we picked up a small brown bottle of Ole Time Woodsman Fly

Coming of Age Stories

Dope, a nasty brown mixture of pine tar and petroleum distillate. The Woodsman's saved our skin as we climbed our first 46ers during the buggiest month of the Adirondack year.

The night of the black flies kicked off my 46er summer. The 46 high peaks of New York's Adirondack Mountains were first climbed in 1925 by brothers George and Bob Marshall and their guide, Herbert Clark. Over the years, climbing the 46 trailed and trailless high peaks grew in popularity. A club, the ADK46ers, has for many years kept a list of climbers who successfully complete all forty-six peaks. According to the club's records, I was the 377th person to complete the feat on August 27, 1966, along with my earliest hiking buddies, Jay Sulzberger and Jack Macintosh.

Jay and I were fresh out of high school. With that first successful climb of Giant Peak, and then the Great Range of the Adirondacks, we decided to devote our summer to becoming 46ers. Jay was gangly, a born mathematician, and an outrageously engaging conversationalist. I was the planner of our small team and Jay the cheerleader, endlessly upbeat and full of interesting talk on the trail.

Charles A. Bookman | **The World Has Changed**

His gift for gab served us well early in our adventure. Faced with a rainy day, we checked into the Adirondack Mountain Club's Adirondack Loj, in the heart of the mountains. Jay engaged a fellow guest, Jack Macintosh, a physics professor from Wesleyan University, in conversation. The mathematician and the physics professor hit it off. Age forty-three, Jack was a very experienced long-distance hiker. Jay and I brought enthusiasm to match Jack's experience. Telling tales of the trail, we realized that we shared the objective of climbing all the 46ers that summer. We resolved to knock off two of the most difficult, trailless Street and Nye mountains, the very next day.

Street and Nye were notable for the thick blowdown that impeded passage up their steep slopes. The blowdown was the result of a powerful winter storm in 1950 that caused a massive downing of trees. Winds up to a hundred miles an hour devastated large swaths of the Adirondacks. According to one report, "The trees were laid in an intense jumble on the ground, hanging on nearby trees, and piled one atop the other."

Over the years young spruces grew up in between the blowndown trees, making an impenetrable forest mass that required hours of painstakingly picking your way over logs and through tangles in order to make any progress at all. We climbed on fallen timber, shoving our way through spruce thickets, swatting at bugs, and climbing ever higher for hour upon hour. Occasionally, the spruce grew so thick we lost visual contact with each other. We would call as we climbed, "I'm okay. How are you doing?"

"Okay over here."

Despite the heat that day, we reached the summit of the first peak, munched our peanut butter sandwiches, then pushed along the ridge to the second summit. There was not much view on these cursed treed summits and the ridge was no easier going. Signing into the second climbing register of the day, we resolved to climb together through the summer until all three of us reached our goal. Eleven hours later, we returned victorious and enthused to Adirondack Loj.

Camping and climbing throughout the summer, Jay, Jack and I became fast friends. Our trail discussions ranged from Noah Rondeau, the famed hermit of the Adirondacks, to Fermat's theorem, to sauropods, to which rocky slopes produced the finest blueberries. Jay had lost his father a few years before, and I suspect Jack filled a void in his life. Perhaps the void-filling was mutual, as Jack was a lifelong bachelor.

The three of us continued our quest two or three days a week over the summer. We climbed the Dix Range, the Santanonis, and Sawteeth. Since Jack had a car, we were able to complete hard to reach outlying peaks like Allen and Couchsacraga. After six weeks, we were almost done, with just a few cleanup climbs. Two months later, Jack completed his 46 peaks. Jay and I finished a week or so after that.

Presidential Traverse, December 1967

The Columbia Mountaineering Club began a traverse of the Presidential Range with nine people at Randolph, New Hampshire, at 10 a.m., December 27, 1967. After a 3,000-foot climb with 70-pound packs that held food and gear for a week of winter camping, we rested the first night near Madison Spring Hut. We climbed Mount Madison the next morning in cloudy weather, then headed along the prominent ridge to Mount Adams. We camped the second night on a small patch of snow beside a steep rock wall a short distance east of Edmands Col in the face of gradually increasing winds, sweeping clouds and a brewing snowstorm. We were about a hundred years away from a small open-ended steel Quonset hut, which could provide emergency shelter. The weather worsened during the evening. By 2 a.m. we became aware of a dangerous situation in which the snow was drifting over our tents faster than it could be swept off. Shouting from one tent to another, we straggled out into the storm. One hiker, Linda, was slow to get dressed and out of her tent, and was nearly buried by the blizzard. We cut her tent open so that she could climb out.

Charles A. Bookman | The World Has Changed

Striking for the emergency shelter would have been reckless. It was a hundred yards off, in the face of gale force winds, with one and a half feet of new drifting snow and no visibility. Relatively mild temperatures encouraged our decision to huddle together in the drifting snow until dawn, when we scrambled over to the shelter.

After the storm front passed, the day grew cloudy and cold. All that day and the following morning, we took turns digging our equipment out from under seven feet of drift. Not even a silk mitten was lost, but the wretched condition of the snow-soaked sleeping bags, boots, and mittens that had been buried caused seven of our party to abandon the expedition and head down that afternoon. Dave Ingalls, our more experienced leader, wanted to continue on, so I volunteered to keep him company.

After watching our companions descend to safety, Dave and I soldiered over Mount Jefferson, and at dusk approached the summit of Mount Washington, the highest peak in New England. The weather was gloriously mild, so mild it lulled us into setting up camp right at the summit. We basked in the glow of a glorious sunset and enjoyed a bottle of champagne the evening before New Year's Eve.

The weather remained clear right through breakfast the following morning, but not more than ten minutes after we struck the tent, the wind kicked up to gale force. Talk about timing!

Leaning into the wind, we made our way over the range to Mizpah Spring Hut. (The Appalachian Mountain Club huts, oases in summer, are shut tight in winter. Nevertheless, they remain useful markers of progress along the Presidential Range.) Near here, we encountered the first of numerous equipment failures, a broken snow shoe. I repaired it with a pine bough and parachute cord.

Except for spectacular weather conditions on the summit of Jackson with 90 miles per hour winds and below zero conditions, the final two and a half days were agonizingly rough going, with deep unconsolidated powder snow and extreme temperatures at night. Progress was around one and a half miles per day as we waded through the deep snow amid thick stunted spruce trees. The final equipment failure tally was two broken snowshoes and two broken pack frames. In addition, our fingers became frostbitten in the high winds on Mount Jackson.

After six days, we were down to raisins and Cream of Wheat for hot food—if we could cook it. Our patched-up gear was further compromised by the cold and wet. Taking stock, we realized we needed to reach the road the next day, our seventh. Pushing hard late in the afternoon, we followed a frozen creek as it plunged steeply over a series of cataracts. At one point, I jumped off a small frozen waterfall and broke through the ice below, soaking myself in freezing water up to my waist. The air temperature Was ten degrees. While I struggled out of the stream, Dave stripped off his dry clothes exchanging them for my wet ones. Dave's sacrifice of his personal comfort at that moment may have saved my life. We made camp immediately, eating the last of our Cream of Wheat and raisins.

We reached the highway at Crawford's Notch mid-morning on January 3, 1968. Our car was frozen in a drift. We flagged down a motorist for assistance.

Dix Range 1968

The following winter, I set my sights on traversing the Adirondacks' Dix Range from Keene Valley to Elk Lake. Rarely done in winter, this trek would involve three nights deep in the mountains and a long walk south on the unplowed road that connects Elk Lake to the state highway. Along the way we would follow the Bouquet River and then tag three summits—Dix, South Dix, and East Dix. (East Dix has since been renamed Grace peak, for Grace Hudowalski, the long-time record-keeper for the ADK46ers.) While I don't recall all of the participants, my friends Jay Sulzberger and Peter Harnik participated, along with several companions from the Columbia Mountaineering Club, including Bob Marcynszyk, a football player.

The weather gods shined on us as we snowshoed up the Bouquet River, and made our first camp in the trees. The next day we tagged summits and camped near the summit of South Dix. All was going well.

There remained the descent down to Elk lake and then the long walk out. Somewhere on the descent, while side-hilling on the ridge, Bob the football player stopped to adjust his gear. He lost control of his pack, which slid at least three hundred feet down on hard packed snow.

"What do I do now?" Bob asked.

"Go fetch it," I said.

This may not sound like much but dropping three hundred feet and climbing back up again is an hour-long ordeal on the third day of a winter expedition. Bob seethed for the rest of the day. The rest of the team remained in good spirits, however, even with the long walk out on the fourth day.

The winter traverse of the Dix Range was an ambitious undertaking. I was proud that I led the team with no serious incidents. The football player withdrew from mountain activities, however, and my friend Peter also gave up snow camping.

More Winter Adventures

As my friend Jay and I continued our winter adventures, with his usual gregariousness, somewhere Jay had met a filmmaker who wanted to make a documentary about ice climbing in Huntington's Ravine on the flank of Mount Washington. Huntington's Ravine is famous for its giant ice waterfalls that beckon climbers from all over the country. The Harvard Mountaineering Club maintains a cabin nearby, a two mile walk from Pinkham Notch.

The filmmaker needed a crew, so I made supporting him a project for the Columbia Mountaineering Club. Improbably, every weekend from late December 1969 until the end of February 1970, on Friday nights two carloads of winter campers drove to Pinkham Notch from New York City, a trip that could take up to nine hours depending on weather. Arriving around midnight, we would load packs with camping and movie-making gear and

Coming of Age Stories

trudge up to the Harvard Cabin, arriving at around 2 a.m. Our arrival would inevitably wake everyone up.

The movie-making gear was not trivial. There were multiple 16 millimeter cameras, lens sets, tripods, light reflectors, and "Battery belts," bandoliers of NICAD batteries that were state of the art at the time. Rising at 6 a.m., we would cut through the ice at a nearby stream for water, make oatmeal, then head out to the ice cliffs. We would generally be on-site and setup by 9 a.m.

In addition to the movie-making gear, we also carried ice climbing gear, including multiple ropes, ice screws, and carabiners. Roy Kligfield, an adept ice climber though still in his teens, led the ice climbing and starred in the movie.

We actually shot several hundred feet of film, even with the short daylight winter hours, horrible weather conditions in what turned out to be a record snow year, and improbable logistics. I have no idea what happened to the footage.

I have one further memory of the ice climbing movie. The movie maker (his name has been overtaken by time) invited us to a New Year's Eve party in SOHO. The rumor was that German filmmaker Werner Herzog would make an appearance. He never did.

There were many other expeditions with climbing buddies Arno Vosk, Larry Brooks, and others. I retired most of my winter gear after I left the New York-New England area in 1974, but I still made occasional forays. In 1996, I took my two sons, then late teenagers, up the Mount Washington carriage road. We made the summit on a spectacular winter day.

I continue to snowshoe and occasionally wear crampons in the Pacific Northwest. I have even camped on snow while climbing the big volcanoes, but I left behind the serious winter camping, where you melt snow for water and worry endlessly about condensation and frostbite, when I left the New England area. My private museum of antique mountaineering gear remains in my basement as a reminder of another time and place. Someday I may part with the equipment, but the memories of bitter cold and close companions will remain forever.

Charles A. Bookman | **The World Has Changed**

Ever since these long ago early adventures, I have continued to find solace in the woods with great trail companions. In the frontispiece of an early Adirondack trail guidebook, opposite a photo of a drenched hiker in a poncho, the caption read, "It wasn't all done in fair weather." In fair weather and foul, a succession of trail companions has carried me—and I them—across decades of heart-thumping adventure and enthralling scenery. Babbling brooks, rustling leaves and flower-filled meadows are great accompaniments to endless interesting conversation about the mountains and molehills of our lives.

Chapter 5

Way Out West 1967

In the dead of winter in New York City, I filled out the yard-long federal form 171, the standard form for federal employment, which even anyone seeking temporary summer work needed to fill out. My application resulted in summer employment on a wilderness trail crew in the Pecos Ranger District of the Santa Fe National Forest, outside (way outside) Santa Fe, New Mexico. In late spring, I boarded a Boeing 727 in New York, then changed in Dallas, TX to a Trans Texas DC-3. The DC-3 stopped at Abilene and Lubbock, Texas then at Clovis, New Mexico before reaching Santa Fe.

The De Vargas Hotel shared its block with the Greyhound Bus Terminal. For $7.50, I got a room with a lumpy, coin-operated vibrating bed and a radio. The sound track included loudspeaker announcements next door of arriving and departing buses to Phoenix, Arizona and Oklahoma City, Oklahoma, with way stations in-between. After the announcements woke me up, I dined on an early breakfast of tortillas, eggs, and green chili in the De Vargas Hotel cafeteria.

Toting my backpack next door, I paid eighty-two cents to ride the Denver bus twenty-five miles east to the village of Pecos, New Mexico alongside the brawling Pecos River. Alighting at the crossroads in the center of town, I noticed a diner, a gas station, and a small motel. A tall moose of a guy was milling around the gas station after the bus pulled away. The moose, Gary, another summer Forest Service recruit, hailed from Utah.

Gary and I walked a short distance down the road to sign our enrollment forms at the ranger station. Everyone was bilingual, but most of the banter was in Spanish. Then we grabbed lunch at the diner, got a double room at the motel, and whiled away the afternoon walking around the village, where tumbledown adobe shacks rented for $38 a month.

Pecos, New Mexico

Pecos, New Mexico seemed to be two towns, one Anglo, the other Chicano. Anglo Pecos straddled the highway with two general stores, the diner where I ate, the motel where I slept, and a couple of bars, such as Stanley's. East Pecos, the Chicano neighborhood, sprawled on the other side of the river. The Chicanos had their own shops and watering holes, such as the Lone Star Bar. Young men cruised in their trucks on Friday nights. Knifings in the 864-person town were common. I was warned not to enter the Lone Star Bar because the previous summer, a Forest Service seasonal worker received a nasty knife gash across his forehead, a broken windshield, and a torn bumper on his car. He was fired the next day for causing trouble.

Pete, the cook at the diner described how Native Americans have occupied the upper Pecos for many centuries because of its good water. Historic pueblo ruins lie just off the road south of town. He opined as well that the fate of the West during the American Civil War might have been decided at nearby Glorieta Pass, where Union forces turned back Confederates in March 1862.

Race tensions were flaring all over New Mexico that summer. The week before I arrived, armed Chicanos had raided the county courthouse in remote (but not very far away) Tierra Amarilla in an effort to resurrect old Mexican land grants that had been ignored in the mid-nineteenth century when the young United States replaced Spain and its vassal Mexico as the territorial sovereign. Reies Tijerina, a Chicano firebrand, had led the raid on Tierra Amarilla. Just days earlier near Pecos, young men briefly seized several children of tourists, telling them that Tijerina was their uncle. Because of the incident with the children, the tourist business—largely camping and fishing—dropped by a third, according to Pete.

Orientation. Eight a.m. Monday morning, Rex Hargraves, the lead ranger, packed eight summer recruits—half Spanish speaking, half English speaking—into the back of his Dodge truck and drove the rough hour-long trip up to Panchuela Ranger Station. Panchuela marked the end of the road, 21 miles and 1200 vertical feet up from Pecos. Perched on a knoll beside Jack's Creek at 8,000 feet elevation, the ranger station consisted of a log cabin bunkhouse, a barn, and a corral for horses and mules. It served as the jumping off point for the Pecos Wilderness, a vast extension of the Rocky Mountains where Ponderosa pine trees and aspen groves gird bold, bare rock summits. The verdant forest provides food and shelter for abundant herds of deer, elk, and mountain sheep. Trout teem in the creeks. Blue jays, hawks, eagles, grouse, and flocks of distinctive yellow and black tanagers fill the trees and sky.

We saddled up soon after we arrived, then rode three miles to our first work site. A contract crew had blasted a rough trail around a rock abutment, and we were there to finish the job. I rode a mule known as "Little Blue" or "Bronco Blue," depending on his mood. Blue carried the bronco nickname because he tended to buck when going downhill. Heading down the trail at the end of the day, everyone waited gleefully for the moment when the city boy would get bucked off. The mule behind me, a black leviathan by the name of Ray, got frisky with Little Blue until the little mule kicked Ray in the teeth. Still descending, we reached a steep section where my mule was sure to buck. By that time, the cinch around his plump middle had come loose and when he kicked, the saddle with me on it slid over his neck. I landed on my feet in front of that little mule much to the amusement of my co-workers.

Poor me, but also poor Ray. The old hands had many Ray stories. One time Ray got frisky with a horse, so one of the hands attacked Ray's prodigious mule member with a curry comb. Another time, Ray acted up with the blacksmith, who kneecapped him with a claw hammer. One morning in the corral, I attempted to coax Ray into his harness unsuccessfully with a carrot. The crew boss then whacked the mule on the behind with a two-by-four. "That's how you get his attention," he said.

That was my orientation to New Mexico, the "Land of Enchantment." The afternoon in the village, the ride in the pick-up truck, and the banter with my new colleagues, both cowboys and Chicanos, made it crystal clear that I was not in the big city! Language was an obvious difference. Nearly everyone I worked with, both regular and summer Forest Service employees, was bilingual. Down in the valley, in Pecos, the locals in front of their modest adobe houses, who still cooked tortillas with a wood-burning stove, greeted me in English while talking with their neighbors in Spanish. At the bunkhouse, an hour above the village, there would be two work crews, one Anglo, the other Chicano, with much bilingual bantering and some rivalry.

Even with the cultural differences, my co-workers and I had a lot in common. Most of us Anglos were in college and whether we were pursuing a degree in forestry or English literature, we took our studies seriously. The differences stemmed from upbringing and outlook. I knew how to drive a taxi cab in New York City; my cowboy co-workers could harness a mule and ride long days in the saddle. The bunkhouse definitely attracted big egos. There seemed to be little tolerance of differences. I came in for a hefty share of teasing, some good-natured, some not. That made for interesting poker games in the evenings; playing cards (and losing a little) helped me fit in.

Coming of Age Stories

We undertook three kinds of work as the summer wore on. At Panchuela, on the edge of the Pecos Wilderness, we saddled up every morning and rode out to a work site. Some days, we worked on trails. At other times, we improved fish habitat in streams. In another part of the Santa Fe National Forest, outside the wilderness area, we spent long days reseeding logged-over mountainsides. There, we slept in wall tents and cooked over a campfire. We also fenced water holes and burned juniper bushes in cattle country on the hot, high Glorieta Mesa, a remote tract of open range in the southern part of the Santa Fe National Forest. On the mesa, we slept in an isolated bunkhouse with no shade and no running water.

At Work. We made stream improvements the first week on nearby Jack's Creek and Holy Ghost Creek. The idea was to place log weirs to widen and deepen the pools to improve trout habitat. We used the mules to drag large ponderosa logs across the cold, clear, swift-flowing creeks to make the impoundments. We also cleaned up the streambanks, removing old beer cans and other fishing litter. Pete Santos directed the stream improvement work. Pete had real Chicano attitude. "Ohhhkayyy boysss," he'd say. "We work for two hours den fuck dee dawggg. Heh? Nobody cares, nobody knows."

There were light moments at Panchuela. Bored and fidgety one evening, as we were going down to the barn, an unlucky chipmunk crossed our path then darted down a drain pipe. A cowboy co-worker tied a burlap sack over one end of the pipe and then rammed a huge stick down the other, forcing the chipmunk into the bag. Someone else tied off the sack and started smashing it against the side of the barn. Others pelted the bag with rocks and boards. When we opened the bag to inspect the chipmunk's bloody remains, we found that the crafty little rascal had never been in the bag in the first place!

Planting pine tree seeds proved tedious, tiring work. Eutemio was in charge. He was an ornery Chicano with a sour stomach and a smirk. Piling into the back of his green Forest Service truck, we rode twenty miles on forest roads deep into logged-

Charles A. Bookman | The World Has Changed

over mountain slopes. Another crew had erected two white canvas wall tents and generally made camp, which included a capacious fireplace and plenty of firewood stacked from the recent timber cutting.

Before us, seventy acres of tangled stumps stretched to the ridgeline and beyond. Eutemio gave us our marching orders: walk seven feet, stoop and plant, repeat. All day long. He passed out rubber gloves. "Don't lick your fingers," he admonished as the seeds had been treated with rat poison. He neglected to mention that we would rip our pants, tear our shirts, and skin our shins, knees, and elbows while clambering over the desolate, brushy ground.

Playing for time, we discussed whether it would be easier to plant up and down or across the slope. After much palaver, we decided to contour. Next, we debated how to use the red, white and blue plastic markers we had been issued to indicate where we had planted. Someone said the decision should be based on which color shows up best, but red blended with the dead pine needles, blue with the sky, and white was camouflaged against clouds and open spaces. In the end, we went patriotic, alternating rows of red, white, and blue.

Maybe I licked my fingers. I don't recall. But I developed a fever and grew faint. So I spent the first afternoon in camp. Although I wasn't planting seeds, I still had to fend off bugs from no-see-ums to hornets that mistook me for a corpse. Returning to planting was a breeze after battling the bugs.

Eutemio and his sidekick, Pete Santos, took it easy while we summer workers planted the seedlings. Pete taught us a little Spanish, starting with the basics. "Ay cabrano" translates loosely to "son of a bitch." Cingatumadre needs no translation. Pella mella does, "Peel your dick." Pete was a good man.

We took turns cooking over the campfire. After supper around the fire in the dying light before turning in, we swapped yarns. During my turn, I noticed a woolly caterpillar crawling out of the spaghetti pot. That prompted one of the cowboys to make up a story.

Coming of Age Stories

"Dear Mommy and Daddy," he began. "Guess what Ol' Charlie did today. You remember me telling you about the time he swallowed peach halves whole because they taste better that way, and how Monday night, he picked up the portable heater to move it and spilled diesel fuel over his sleeping bag and stank up the tent? Well tonight he found a caterpillar in the spaghetti pot and said to leave it in for flavor."

I took some small solace in being referred to as "Ol' Charlie." The diesel fumes permeated my sleeping bag for the rest of the summer.

A large, enameled coffee pot hung over the fire. To make "cowboy coffee," we filled an athletic sock with coffee grounds and tossed it in to float around in the boiling water. There were the inevitable jokes about whether the sock was clean, or whether the coffee had a certain indefinable tang from prior use.

We'd gotten the hang of campfire cooking by the final day of tree planting, but it takes a little longer to make breakfast over a fire, so we didn't start planting until almost 9 a.m. At 10:30, it was time for our contract-guaranteed, mid-morning ten minute break. We slogged again with the back breaking labor until lunch at noon. We broke up the tedium on the hillside with the occasional joke.

At 1:00 p.m. we were supposed to resume activities, so we discussed the prospects for a productive afternoon. Most days, clouds gathered a little after lunchtime and it often rained with accompanying thunder and lightning. "I don't want to get way the heck out there only to have the clouds open up on me," Ramon, one of the supervisors, would say. "We'd better stay here until the clouds blow over. That way we'll know for sure." Ramon then would crawl under a tree and drop off to sleep. The sun would often shine again by 1:30 but Ramon often would continue to snore, deep satisfied animal snores.

Ramon was 25, blond and fiercely proud of his Mexican ancestry. "My name," he says, "Is Ramon L. Roybal. My father and my father's father were Mexicans, and that's the way it should be."

"What's the 'L' in your middle name stand for?" I asked him. "Lazy," he replied with an impish grin. Ramon had served in the

U.S. Navy. "You know what I learned in this man's Navy? To pet the dog. You know, gold brick. Waste time." And there he would be, beneath that tree, snoring in the sunshine. The morning seed planting must have tired him out.

On our final day replanting the mountainside, we returned to work at 2:15 p.m. but ran out of marking tape at 3 p.m. Ramon pointed out that it would take a full half hour to walk to the vehicles and another hour to navigate the fire roads back to the ranger station, so we'd better get started, he said. "I didn't drink no beer last weekend," he explained. "That's how come I know." So, after dawdling back to the vehicles, coasting along the fire roads down to the valley road, taking a short detour through the dude ranches to ogle the new arrivals, stopping at the store, and another general colloquy at the filling station, we reached the ranger station at 5:00 p.m. Our week planting seed and sleeping in wall tents already behind us.

Digging Fence Posts, Glorieta Mesa

Several miles south of Pecos, the opposite direction from Panchuela, lies a high, flat, hot plateau known variously as Rowe

Coming of Age Stories

Mesa or Glorieta Mesa. At 9,000 feet, the top of the mesa juts up 2,000 feet above the Pecos River valley. Range grass covers this high land. It's a tough, hardy, tawny colored fiber. Piñon trees, a scrappy, scratchy version of juniper, dot the grasslands. Now and then a beautiful yellow or pink desert flower or a cactus breaks the sea of sedge.

The glaring desert sun rises about 6 a.m. and sets about 9 p.m. In between, it bakes the life out of everything that moves. Bleached cow bones litter the range. The ground has hardened into cement. On those rare days when rain clouds pass overhead, the cement cracks into huge arroyos. Water runs everywhere, ending inevitably in a huge puddle, to be baked out of existence within an hour. Only the arroyos remain, scars on the landscape.

The mesa is more purgatory than hell because life abounds even under the harsh conditions. We encountered weasels, rattlesnakes, mountain lions, bears, and coyotes. Stinging red ants scurried everywhere. Their three-foot mounds looming like blackheads on the face of the plateau.

In the midst of this, the Forest Service maintained a cabin, reachable only by heavy duty vehicles that could make it up to the mesa. There's no water other than man-made stock holes, little shade, plenty of red ants, and rattlesnakes.

Three of us, Eutemio, Bill, and I spent a week at the bunkhouse building fences around water holes. Each of us drank two gallons a day and took salt tablets to ward off heat stroke. We received five-dollars' daily hardship pay.

At Play. Historic New Mexican towns are built around a central plaza. Sometimes I spent the weekend hanging around Santa Fe's plaza, where I would meet other young people, some local, some not. Other weekends, I hitched or drove to Taos, where I did pretty much the same thing. A couple of weekends, I stayed behind at the Panchuela bunkhouse in order to take long hikes deep into the Pecos Wilderness.

After work on Fridays, I would catch a ride or take the Greyhound to town (later in the summer, I drove my car). In Santa

Charles A. Bookman | The World Has Changed

Fe, I checked into the De Vargas Hotel, washed up, ate a good New Mexican supper in the hotel cafeteria, listened to the radio until dusk, then headed to the plaza with my sketch pad. Eventually someone my age, sometimes a woman, often on the hippie end of the social spectrum, would take notice. I would ask my new companion to doodle on the pad, and we would talk for a while. One night, I met two sisters from Roswell, New Mexico. Another evening, I met another New York City refugee working for the summer as a waiter. I enjoyed these affirming chance encounters; they were definitely a positive change from the social tensions in the bunkhouse.

One evening, following the sound of laughter, I joined a group of locals in the plaza. Cynthia, heavy set but light and bubbly as ginger ale caught my eye. "I know some people," she said. "A party..."

I walked with her to a small apartment on a nearby side street. From a corner of the living room, I looked over the group. I had joined a mixed crowd, some Anglo, some Chicano. A gallon-jug of vino di tavola, the cheapest of wines, kept the conversation flowing.

"You guracho," a curly headed young man teased. "You're a guracho in the midst of Mexicans. Tough ones at that. Do you know what it means, guracho? Anglo, dirty anglo. Aren't you scared?" He grinned.

"Oh, don't tease the guracho," a guy I had walked over with said. "He's my friend."

"Guracho, you know I just broke out of prison. Are you hippie? Can I tell you about it?"

"Why do I have to be a hippie to hear about your stretch in the pen?" I asked.

"Watch your language, Guracho," he said. "You're Anglo, we're Grease. Last September, they picked me up on possession of marijuana. Spent ninety-four days in the county jail. That county jail, man, it's hard to take. Six cells in the block. No windows. Nothing to do man, but at least all the people in there are clean. Short time, no perverts."

Coming of Age Stories

"My court lawyer said I would probably get off on a first offense, so I walked into court that day all dressed in my Mexican best and chewing gum. The judge didn't like that. 'You've been to Springer twice,' he said. That is the reform school. 'Looks like you didn't learn a thing. I'm sending you to prison. The court orders you to serve six months of a five year sentence. Court adjourned.'"

"You know they are not supposed to hold your juvenile record against you in adult court. But still I went to jail," he said. "But I'm stupid, man. I was there four months and was a trusty. Worked in the kitchen. One day I was taking garbage outside the walls. The sky was so blue. Hadn't seen it in ages. So blue. I started to run and just kept on running With only two months left, man."

"That prison is so bad. The long timers, lifers, haven't had a woman, you know, so the first thing they do is try and make you queer. And if you don't give they'll kill you. Five of them, all with knives, will corner you and tell you to give. Either you give or you knife one of them. It only adds a year to your sentence. If you don't they'll get you. It wasn't that way for me because I've been in those circles all my life. But you know, in New Mexico state pen, a guracho doesn't stand a chance."

"The sheriff caught up with me a few days ago. I go back for the full five years on August 11. I'm on parole now. Correction–breaking parole. This beer in my hand is illegal. These friends of mine here, all from reform school, are illegal. I don't know what I'll do. Maybe Canada or something. But hell, five years from now, I'll be straight, man. Clean!"

Later that evening, I was canoodling with Marie from Jemez pueblo. She seemed willing but my teenage self wasn't making much progress. "Your bra won't come undone," I finally said. "It's glued or something."

"Just a minute," she said looking at me and fiddling under her blouse. At this inopportune moment, my head began to spin with the inevitable denouement. Later, definitely without Marie, having locked myself out of the house, I passed out near the back door. I rose at dawn, cold and damp from the dew and other misfortunes.

The weekend after receiving my first paycheck, I hitchhiked to Albuquerque. I walked into the first used car lot I came to, plunked $50 on the counter and drove away in an eggshell-white 1956 Nash Rambler American that looked like a sack of wet mashed potatoes. If a car can have a limp, the rambler did. The steering column was so bent you could set the wheel in one position and it would stay there. Compounding the imbalanced look and feel, the right side hung lower than the left.

I called the Rambler "Ray" after the cantankerous, infamous mule at Panchuela. Would Ray get me back up the dirt mountain road to Panchuela? Would Ray carry me to Santa Fe and Taos on the weekends? Would he get me home at the end of the summer?

I drove the 140 miles to Taos to see what Ray could do. Ray got 23 miles to the gallon, didn't burn oil or leak transmission fluid, and the tires held air. But the muffler made noise, the brakes squeaked, and I lost the driver side mirror to a kicked-up road stone. Not bad for $100, I thought.

At Taos, I noticed a group of friendly people hanging around the central square (just as I expected). "Hi there," a pretty dark-eyed Indian girl called. "Come join our party." Seven girls were gathered around one guy, all playing drums, bells, guitars. "Tompkins Square West," I thought.

Someone suggested swimming under the stars at a nearby hot spring resort that had fallen on hard times. We piled into the back of a pickup truck with a case of Country Club malt liquor and drove some fifteen miles deep into the arid desert to an abandoned mansion. A string of small pools ran alongside the road, all fed by a hot spring. I climbed up to the very top pool—a tiny eight-foot-square jewel, stripped, and dove in. Legs were everywhere. Hands slithered up legs. It was so dark you couldn't distinguish boys from girls and occasionally someone would shout out "Sorry!"

Patty paddled over to me. She wanted to avoid the mass orgy in the middle of the pool and I was happy to oblige.

Coming of Age Stories

We stayed in the hot pools long enough to satisfy ourselves and wrinkle up. Then we dressed, built a campfire and got very drunk. The Indian girl sang songs.

I spent that night in a three dollar room at the Hotel Traveler. The following morning, the Indian girl invited me to the Taos Pueblo, an active Indian village that supports itself off tourism. I found the visit disappointing. Indian mothers made their children dance for tourists and then pass the hat.

Returning to the Taos Square, I spent the afternoon with my new Indian friends. I picked up an Apache swear word, "Asakanina," which means "Eat shit, go to hell, suck off." We ate sourdough bread with corn cob jelly, washing it down with wine. By dusk, we were drunk enough to resume beating the tom-tom. I drummed, the other guy played the flute and the Indian girls danced and chanted. Our musical antics attracted quite a crowd: hippie girls, ordinary girls, old men, and young toughs. The police showed up but they were friendly, just watching. We drove into the hills then set off fireworks in the dark.

There were two large communes around Taos at the time. New Buffalo was the better known one because it invited tourists in to gawk at its enclave of tepees. The other, Dixon, was an out-of-the-way little village. A girl invited me there one weekend. Sixteen people, including a baby, a dog named Broadway, and Cragmont the cat lived in a four-room adobe house. A large garden out back produced lettuce, corn, squash, radishes, tomatoes, beans, watermelons and marijuana. A huge pot of beans bubbled on the woodburning stove. The beans were accompanied on the table by an indescribably delicious fresh salad.

Dixon was traditional in that the women kept house and cooked while the men worked in the fields. On the weekend I visited, we irrigated the field and leavened our work with mud fights. I enjoyed the communal contrast with my individualistic cowboy weekdays.

The weekends I stayed behind at the bunkhouse, I followed horse trails into the high country. One weekend I headed for nearby 12,400-foot Pecos Baldy. I passed a little tarn at the base of the gaunt, gray rock, a trout filled gem sitting at timberline. Making the final pull up the bare rock to the summit, I passed within ten yards of a herd of big horn sheep. From the top, the Sangre de Christo Range stretched north to 13,000-foot Truchas Peak; to the south, my eyes took in seventy miles of range land, all the way to the Rio Grande and beyond.

Returning from the mountain, a female pheasant fell in step behind me. Ambling together through a moist glen, the bird suddenly stopped and clucked, much like an angered chicken. Looking about, I counted eight other pheasants on both sides of the trail. I offered them some of my raisins.

Further along, kicking a stone down the trail, I heard a tremendous roar over my right shoulder. There on a ledge not more than twenty feet above me stood a Texas Longhorn steer. His hide was tough as the forest, his horns as wide as the trees. He pawed the ground with heavy feet. I made it to the nearest tree in five seconds flat. Discounting the run in with the longhorn and the inevitable afternoon thunderstorm it was a great day.

Summer Rangers at Beatty's Cabin, Pecos, NM

Another weekend hike took me up a steep canyon rising from a fast flowing creek. My destination was Beatty's, a cozy log cabin situated high on a flower-bedecked slope. Several of my range-riding bunkhouse companions had ridden up the day before and welcomed me with a roaring fire and roast chicken dinner. Nearby, three pert little horses munched hay in the corral. At eight p.m., we sat beside the window waiting for deer to graze the lush grass in the meadow. I felt at that moment, in the evening light, midst the flowers and deer, Beatty's Cabin is as close as you can get to heaven on earth.

Endless Summer. The summer of 1967 Scott McKenzie sang "Are you going to San Francisco (with flowers in your hair)?" On the country air waves, Buck Owens crooned "Sam's Place," and Loretta Lynn belted out, "Don't come home a'drinkin (with loving on your mind)." That's what played on the radio in my little Nash Rambler as I left New Mexico and crossed Oklahoma on my way back to New York City.

The car unfortunately didn't make it that far. The U joint that connects the axle to the engine fell out at an intersection in St. Louis, Missouri. I sold the Rambler for $25 to the guy who ran the gas station at the corner where my car became stranded, and I hitchhiked the rest of the way back east.

My body had responded well to the summer's tough work on the trails, in the creeks, on the hillsides, and high on the mesa. Sweat flooded my face, my hands grew tough, and grit covered me from head to toe.

My social game had grown as well. Challenged in the bunkhouse, I searched for ways to communicate with others who "Didn't get me." Over the weekends, in the plazas, I connected with people from very different walks of life—Pueblo Indians, Chicanos, prisoners, back-to-the-landers. Even if I didn't quite fit in, I learned how to get along. I learned that in order to connect, you need to communicate. Put yourself out there. Make the first move. With the perspective of almost six decades, those early lessons and enchanting experiences have served me well.

Chapter 6

Political Awakening 1968

Columbia University's campus erupted in political demonstrations in the spring of my sophomore year. Instigated by the new left, anti-war Students for a Democratic Society (SDS) and sustained by factions ranging from black urban activists to die-hard Maoists, students besieged the campus until the campus administration called in the New York City police. Seven hundred protesters were arrested in a midnight raid. A student-led general strike shut the campus down for the remainder of the semester. The political fire among college students that began at Columbia in 1968 raged around the world. In France, the student revolt quickly evolved into a general strike that paralyzed the country.

The story of student unrest at Columbia University and elsewhere has been told many times. James Kunen (a fellow student)'s book, *The Strawberry Statement* presents the student unrest as a coming-of-age story. Mark Rudd, the SDS leader who led the demonstrations, in his autobiography *Underground* credits his Columbia experience with the personal radicalization

Coming of Age Stories

that led him into domestic terrorism as a leader of the Weather Underground. Filmmaker Paul Cronin's fifteen-hour documentary, *A Time to Stir* emphasizes the role of disaffected black students in the radicalization of the campus.[1] I participated actively in the demonstrations. Recognizing the "Rashomon effect,"[2] where different individuals provide differing perspectives about the same incident, here is my story.

I didn't want to be in college, but the Vietnam War was raging, and with a student deferment from the military draft, being in college kept you out of the war. I had wanderlust bad. I hadn't started collecting stamps in my passport yet but I crisscrossed the country as often as I could. Usually I hitchhiked—I didn't keep a car in New York City until the fall of 1968, and the Columbia strike occurred that spring. Many of my classmates were in the same boat. They didn't want to be in school, but if they had to, they would make the best of the situation, or try to.

The military draft threatened us every day and shaped our lives. We didn't like the war, and our university was helping with the war effort. How was Columbia helping? Roger Hilsman at the School of International Studies (where I took courses) had served as Assistant Secretary of State for Southeast Asia. From State, he helped Secretary of Defense Robert McNamara advocate for "fighting communism" in southeast Asia. The dean of the School of International Affairs (later interim president of Columbia), Andrew Cordier was a Dick Cheney-esque character. At the CIA, Cordier had orchestrated (according to some) the assassination of Patrice Lumumba, a Communist leaning leader of the new republic of the

---

[1] Paul Cronin interviewed me for his documentary. At the time (2014), I happened to be reading a 600-page collection of interviews with Werner Herzog, the filmmaking auteur. The book lay on the coffee table as Cronin set up his equipment. Noticing the book he said, "I see you are reading my book." His name appeared on the cover as the editor. "You are the only person I've ever met who has actually read the book," he said.

[2] Named for Akira Kurosawa's 1950 movie, "Rashomon." The movie examines the meaning of truth as four people recount a murder and rape from their individual perspectives.

Congo. "Bongo Bongo in the Congo" went our chant. Also, "Hey, hey Cordier, how many people did you kill today." Columbia participated in a shadowy partnership between an obscure Defense Department agency and academia, the Institute for Defense Analyses, which hooked up academic professors with war-fighting needs.

Racism played a role as well. With the City's permission, Columbia was building a gym that extended into Morningside Park. The park is a gem today, all cleaned up and surrounded by middle class apartments. In the '1960's, Morningside Park was a no-man's land that separated Columbia on Morningside Heights from Harlem down in the valley. The multi-story gym was to have an opening at the top for students and a separate, second-class gym at the bottom for Harlem. Never the twain would meet.

We protesters were angry about the university's complicity in the war, and its patronizing attitude towards the community (and also its students). Coincident with the annual springtime antics that break out on every college campus, ours turned into days of rage. Each daily demonstration built on the next. On April 10, 1968, Mark Rudd led a contingent of white middle-class students to the site of the gymnasium. The students were loosely affiliated with SDS. SDS, a loose leftist collective with chapters on many college campuses, had grown out of the Civil Rights Movement. The activist Tom Hayden was its driving force.[1] Mark Rudd was one of the local Columbia organizers.

Rudd describes the disorder of the day in his book *Underground* (2009). I attended the rally and heard the speeches, and then I returned to my apartment on West 110th Street, where I studied, cooked dinner, and eventually went to bed.

My friend Robert Spindel called me at 5 a.m. "Charlie," he said. "You won't believe it. We're in the President's Office in Low Library. Come quickly before you can't get in."

---

[1] Tom Hayden would go onto a distinguished civic career in the California State Legislature. He also married the actress and activist, Jane Fonda. His cameo role at Columbia is mentioned in his memoir, Reunion (1988).

Coming of Age Stories

Later that afternoon, after I had left the rally at the gym site, SDS had occupied the university president's office in Low Library, and a contingent of black students had kidnapped the Columbia College dean and taken over Hamilton Hall, the college's headquarters building. Dressing quickly, I walked the short six blocks up to the campus. The door to Low was blocked, but the president's office was on the second floor, which had an open window. Directly below the window was a large black, easily climbable grate. I scampered up the grate, pulled myself up onto the stone ledge, and entered through the open window. The office was jammed with excited students. Over the next day, I helped organize the ingress and egress from the office via the black grate and second floor ledge. This was the right thing to do, especially since I was vice president of the Columbia Mountaineering Club and climbing buildings was a favorite city activity for us at the time. Correct grate- and ledge-climbing practices would also help keep our protest safe, I reasoned. I spent many hours on the ledge over the next few days and in so doing I not only helped hundreds of people and transferred hundreds of bags of provisions. I also had my photo taken by the New York Times, the Daily News, and the New York Post. The trifecta! My mother was mortified.

Students took over other buildings. My friend Robert occupied Avery Hall, home to the School of Architecture, science students and radicals occupied Mathematics Hall; Gary Wasserman (a friend from later in life) joined social science and liberal arts students in Fayerweather Hall. It was a heady time. I eventually moved over to Fayerweather, where I found the people more congenial, perhaps because the protesters there were more middle-of-the-road, favoring non-violence over active resistance. Gary remembers endless polemical discussions about the rightness of our actions and whether the student protesters deserved complete amnesty. I mostly remember discussions about whether the furniture was piled high enough against the doors.

Over in Mathematics Hall, the barricades were more robust than elsewhere. ("Up against the wall" had a very literal mean-

Charles A. Bookman | **The World Has Changed**

Running Supplies Outside the President's Office

ing at the time.) I snuck in through the underground tunnels, thanks to my friend and climbing partner Jack Yatteau, who had an encyclopedic knowledge of the underground tunnel system that connected all campus buildings. Tom Hayden, wearing a white karate robe, came from national SDS to rally the troops. He delivered an impassioned speech about war resistance and the importance of militant action.

Teachers attempted to hold classes for the first few days. I remember being told in geology that we could take the exam or accept a pass for the year. My lab instructor, Steve Connery, a rock climbing pal (and eventual colleague on an oceanographic ship), told me years later that he didn't understand why I would opt for a pass in a course where I was earning an A. But that particular spring, opting for a pass and not a letter grade constituted a political act.

When the police finally entered the buildings after 2 a.m. on April 30, they were itching to bust the heads of the upper-class kids gone wild. A thousand of the New York Police Department's finest men in blue had waited in buses just off campus for the signal to go in. In nonviolent Fayerweather Hall, we sat on the floor waiting for the inevitable onslaught. Our political discourse—about the war, racism, whether to fight for amnesty for the protesters—continued endlessly into the night. Some tied wet handkerchiefs around their faces to lessen the effects of tear gas. We sang, "We Shall Overcome."

Coming of Age Stories

I am not sure whether you would call the police behavior a riot, but chaos ensued.[1] As far as I could tell, every protester got bonked on the bean with a truncheon. We wore the blood streaming from our scalps as a badge of honor.

Cowed and bowed by the truncheon, the police herded us out of the buildings onto the street on the east side of the campus. There we were loaded into buses and taken downtown for arrest and booking. Paul Marks, dean of the medical school and a family friend, spotted me in the line. Wearing a medical arm band, he steered me to a waiting ambulance, which took me not to police headquarters at 100 Center Street but to St. Luke's Hospital in Harlem. I was ushered into the emergency room and then simply walked out another door and home to West 110th Street.

Most of my friends were in the buildings. Over in Avery Hall, the police pushed my friend Robert down a flight of stairs. He left Columbia that summer for Reed College in Portland, Oregon. Friends in other buildings reported similar rough handling.

Other students—Including the future US Attorney General Robert Barr, and future Governor of New Hampshire Judd Gregg—were involved in counter demonstrations in favor of maintaining order on campus.

The siege turned into a strike, and the campus shut down entirely for the remainder of the semester. These days, when we wonder where the outrage is—against current wars, our health care system that keeps the poor sicker than the rich, and our broken politics—it is hard to think back to a time when we felt we could change the world. Where is the anger today? Perhaps we are too busy getting ahead to be angry. Or perhaps we are just too busy with our bread and circuses.[2]

---

[1] Paul Cronin's movie delves into the attitude of the police, which reflected class as well as political differences.

[2] As this book took shape in the spring of 2024, students protesting the Israeli War in Gaza had disrupted college campuses across the United States. As in 1968, demonstrations at Columbia were among the first and most strident in the nation.

Chapter 7

Summer of Love 1968

"If you're going to San Francisco, be sure to wear flowers in your hair" was the anthem. I never lingered in San Francisco that summer, but I spent considerable time on California's coastal "Hippie Highway." I hopscotched from Idaho to Washington, to California, then to Wyoming and ultimately back East. I worked, I climbed, I met people from all walks of life. A little spot of beach just south of Carmel, California holds a big place in my heart.

Journey West

After classes ended prematurely midst the chaos of the student uprising at Columbia University, I headed west. I had a connection for a summer job at the *Idaho Statesman* in Boise; the editor was my father's war buddy. I staked my taxicab earnings on a one-way airplane ticket. When I called from the airport, the receptionist told me that the editor had suffered a massive heart attack and was in the hospital. After talking to him briefly,

I concluded that he was in no position to help. I made a brief trip downtown to the editorial offices where no one knew anything about my summer internship. By mid-afternoon, I was hitchhiking west.

A day later, I washed up like so many others on the Pacific coast in Seattle, Washington. Seattle had cheap lodgings in those days (some of the signs remain a curiosity in historic Pioneer Square). I got a room at the Hotel Astor at 8th and Pine. (The block was razed in 1985 for a convention center.)

The city looked down and out (parts of town still look down and out). The University of Washington was more familiar territory. The stores and the women on University Avenue looked more congenial. I thought maybe I could base myself in Seattle, at least for the summer.

I had only the vaguest of plans—maybe set chokers on a logging crew. Whatever the next move, I would need a car. I rode the bus to West Seattle to look at a $125 car but there was no car. The owner had sold it out from under me. I took another bus over to the Magnolia neighborhood to look at a 1954 Ford for sale for $100. The owner had just graduated from high school. He spent the afternoon with me, helping to obtain insurance and registration.

I left Seattle that evening, headed for Mount Rainier "for the weekend." A rainstorm caught me along highway 410. The rain poured down. The windshield wipers didn't work. The car chugged along through the wet until it didn't. I took the plates off, then crossed the highway intending to hitch a ride back to Seattle.

On The Hippie Highway

A 1952 Chevy pickup pulled over. "Hop in, get dry," the driver, Jim Darcy, said. Jim had been a high school athlete but now considered himself a hippie. He was headed to Carmel, California to get his mojo back—and possibly his girl. I went along for the ride.

Charles A. Bookman | **The World Has Changed**

House at 19th & Pine, Pacific Grove, CA

We headed west to the Pacific, and drove the slow road down the coast through the night. Jim's girlfriend Kristin had left him. I had left the East. He said life was a game. I said we play for keeps. We grew high on good talk and lack of sleep. Twenty-four hours later, we pulled into his friend's abode in Pacific Grove, California. Jim's boyhood friend Wayne worked as a pastry chef at Highlands Inn, just south of Carmel, in the area known as "The Highlands." Wayne had married a girl named Cathy because she was pregnant by a guy who'd left and because he wanted to. Cathy had a friend who lived with them, Cindy from Seattle. Cindy's boyfriend ran out six weeks before Jim arrived. They all lived together in a little green house on the corner of Nineteenth Street and Pine Avenue in Pacific Grove.

From the moment they passed around their first pipe of gold, Cathy and Wayne were telling Cindy it was high time to stop crying over her lost boyfriend. Jim picked up with Cindy and moved into the little green house. Cindy brought out her guitar and taught Jim a riff or two. "Back in Seattle all I did with Kristen and her friends was watch their intellectual games and social antics," Jim told me. "Down here I can grow."

Two weeks later, Jim was strumming a $200 Goya guitar. He'd gotten it in trade for his truck, which had died. He said he would be leaving soon. Cindy took it all right.

Coming of Age Stories

Pregnant Cathy was picking up vibes. She knew Wayne would go too, and she cried a lot. Wayne was hounded by the situation and also by the Federal Bureau of Investigation, which was interested in him for inciting a riot at a draft rally in Oakland, California. So, he and Jim planned secretly to take off for Canada.

When Jim and Cindy (Cathy stayed home weeping) went to Highlands Inn to pick up Wayne from work, Kristin was there too. She had realized the only way to get Jim back was to *get him back*. Retrieve him. So she had hitchhiked down from Seattle.

Jim learned then that you can't just walk away from a moment. Sometimes you can't turn your back. That thing he thought he could find on the coast couldn't be found until he was ready for it. So, he embraced the girl he'd run away from. Jim's friend Wayne realized that a wife was for keeps.

So, Wayne and Cathy and Jim and Kristin all left the little green house in Pacific Grove on the corner of 19th and Pine for Canada. Let us hope everyone was happy for a time, even Cindy, the girl outside the circle.

With the help of the residents in the Pacific Grove house, I made my way in Monterey. They steered me to the State Employment Office. "I need a job," I said to the lady behind the counter, rhinestones on her rims.

"Job skills?" she asked.

I froze. Twelve years of school, two years of college. Job skills? Readin', Writin' Rithmetic, what else? I had built trail in the Forest Service the summer before. "I can use a hoe," I said. The employment lady smiled and explained that hoeing work was available in the lettuce fields in the Salinas Valley. All I had to do was to meet the labor contractors at 5:00 in the morning in downtown Salinas, a short twenty miles away. The pay was okay, the hours long I would do all right, she assured me.

I weighed my options. I could stay at the house in Pacific Grove. In those hippie times, no one would kick you out. But I felt awkward. No one had invited me, and relationships seemed strained between the people who knew each other, not to mention the guy from the east coast who dropped in from the road. I could work at the Highlands Inn, where several of the house people worked. It was a resort hotel just south of Monterey. It hugged the side of a rugged mountain rising sheer out of the sea. There seemed to be lots of work in the hotels around there. Pay was poor, but work was available. Or, I could try the lettuce fields. Visions of Steinbeck jumped in my head. How could I get as far as Steinbeck country and not try farmwork?

The hitch across the divide to the Salinas Valley was a snap. I rode over at dusk and unrolled my sleeping bag behind a Dairy Queen. I willed myself to wake before dawn, so that I would be able to catch the labor contractor and the ride out to the field in an old school bus. The cold gray light of dawn found me shivering in Salinas. The first person I met on the street looked about as drifty as I felt, and he hadn't been to sleep during the night, spending his time drinking instead. I asked him where I could find the bus to the fields. He said, "Where's my car? I can't find my car?"

I helped him look for his car to no avail. In the process, we passed the courthouse steps and stumbled on the migrant workers loading onto the school buses to the fields. I signed on and hopped aboard. I felt awkward. Everyone else, I realized had done this before. Everyone else had calluses and hats to keep the sun at bay. Everyone else was Mexican and spoke Spanish.

The rows of lettuce stretched to the horizon. We all started in a line, each to a row. I weeded and weeded with the hoe, head down, long chop, short chop, long chop, short chop. I thought I was doing pretty good until I looked up. The Mexicans were at the end of the row already and I had progressed only about a third of the way. By the time I finished my row, the Mexicans had caught up with me again, but they had finished three rows. The gringo jokes were starting. The boss man was on my case because I was too slow. The workers were teasing me because I was so obviously out of place. I knocked off about ten in the morning, just walked out of the field to the highway, stuck out my thumb and headed back to Pacific Grove.

Coming of Age Stories

Carmel State Beach on the Hippie Highway

I have reflected on this experience many times over the years. We admired communal, socialistic endeavors in the 1960s. Together, we believed, the workers and the intelligentsia were going to overthrow the oppressors. Students stood with the grape workers and helped them organize. My cousin went to Cuba to harvest sugar cane. Friends joined Vista to work on Indian reservations or went to Mississippi to help sharecroppers register to vote. I went into the lettuce fields and wondered what the hell I was doing there. It has colored my politics ever since.

Just south of the Carmel peninsula, snuggled at the base of Point Lobos is a small state beach beside Highway One. I called the beach home for the next six weeks.

I hired on at Highlands Inn, where everyone from the Pacific Grove house worked. It's perched on a sea cliff a short mile further down the coast highway, just beyond Point Lobos State Park. George Romney, Vincent Price, and Natalie Wood stayed at Highlands Inn. I earned minimum wage, $1.65 an hour, doing general outdoor labor.

Charles A. Bookman | **The World Has Changed**

My life for the next weeks alternated between toiling at the inn and sleeping on the beach. At the inn, I split firewood for 101 fireplaces. I drove the garbage truck, and with another laborer constructed a 20-foot-tall masonry obelisk by the highway to hold the large, handmade "Highlands Inn" wooden sign. The owner of the inn, a Scotsman, deserved his reputation for thrift. He paid minimum wage, refused reasonable requests for advancement, and provided workers bed and board at usurious costs. Staff turnover was, as a result, quite high. I replaced the garbageman who had just quit after working two and a half years without a raise. The executive chef had just been fired for his rather "unorthodox" hiring procedures for waitresses. Only five days had passed since the assistant chief houseboy and a bellhop were fired for partying in a vacant room late at night. The man who had split firewood before me had been fired for forgetting to latch the tailgate on the truck and dropping a pickup-load of wood on the steep roadway. While I worked there, a carpenter quit because he thought a union painter should be given better work than ditch digging. Staff turnover at Highlands Inn was high, but morale was not low. The quick-change style of staffing had become the local joke. Having worked for and quit Highlands Inn entered you into a fraternity of ne'er-do-wells.

Highlands Inn, Carmel Highlands, CA

Coming of Age Stories

Nighttime on the beach, I collected driftwood for a fire. As dusk settled around in the evening chill, pilgrims wandered over from the hippie highway. People contributed whatever they had to my stewpot, and there was always weed, guitars, women, even dogs. Sometimes a woman would sit next to me. After small talk around the fire, she would lean in. On the other side of the fire, there might be another girl and a companion.

One night, under a half-moon, by the fire, a couple across from me gave each other back rubs. Next morning, after the girl had left, I asked the guy how his evening had gone. "Hand job," he said.

"Did you enjoy it?"

"Physical release," he said. I asked him if the girl was nice. He said he didn't even know her name. The conversation reminded me of one of Groucho Marx's quips about the other sex, "The screwing you get isn't worth the screwing you get."

Another evening, a couple dressed as gypsies sat by my fire. They had a baby. When the baby was hungry, gypsy mama opened her simple black blouse and the babe latched onto her breast. The baby's eyes lit in the firelight! His cheeks burned rosy bright, brighter than the breast he suckled. The babe smiled as he suckled. Gypsy mama smiled at me. I smiled back and played with the babe's wispy hair. "Instant love," gypsy mama mumbled.

A long, straight-haired young man and his wiry tawny terrier stopped by my fire one night. "What's the dog's name?"

"Hookah."

"And what's your name?"

"I'm Ralph."

"I'm Charlie." We shook hands.

"It's a pretty beach," Ralph said. "Hookah doesn't talk much."

"No, she's pretty quiet for a little dog. I'll bet she thinks a lot, though."

"But sometimes she'll get in rappin-yappin mood and usually late at night—"

"Yeah, at 3 a.m., probably when you have to be up at 5—"

"She'll wake up everyone around except me. But she's a good old dog. Like a couple of nights ago five of us were sleeping on the porch of my friend Joe's cabin. Hookah gets to rappin-yappin and made everyone go inside except me."

"Should have put the dog in."

"What sign are you? I'm Scorpio."

"Pisces. Today's my day to make a decision but I haven't made one yet. Deciding whether to drift or to swim."

I decided to drift mid-summer, to go climbing in the Palisades Region of the Sierra Nevada, up behind Big Pine, California. I became one more temporary statistic in the endless roster of former Highlands Inn employees.

Mountain Interlude

I had a vague plan to meet climbing friends at the trailhead for the Middle Palisades in California's Sierra Nevada mountains. In those days, long before cell phones and in an area where the nearest pay phone was twelve miles away, communication was a little difficult. Confident in the plan, I waited for my friends. After two days, I hoofed the twelve miles to the nearest pay phone in Big Pine. I learned that my climbing friends were still in New York. Two of them had court appearances related to the Columbia uprising. They planned to come west, to the Tetons in Wyoming, in mid-August, after court obligations were behind them. I caught a ride back to my camp with Carol and Steve, students at the University of California at Los Angeles (UCLA). They were camping in search of spiritual renewal before summer session. They dropped by my campsite for Rice-a-Roni and chocolate pudding.

The next day, I scrambled steeply up for an hour to the base of a prominent jam crack that ran diagonally left to right in the cliff high up on the ridge. The view from the crack was incredible. Across the steep Big Pine Creek canyon rose North and Middle Palisades. With their glaciers, the horizon was all shadows and crags.

Coming of Age Stories

Back in camp in late afternoon, I walked over to a nearby pickup camper. Three guys had just been laid off from the potash mine in Trona, California, a desert dry lake bed. Summer temperatures in Trona hit 100 degrees or more but the mine pays $2.93 per hour for manual labor. If it hadn't been for the layoffs, working there might have been a possibility.

The four of us downed Coors beer, ate hot dogs, then settled into a poker game. Pete, the loudmouth, had incredible luck. He kept pulling two pairs in a variation of five card stud that they liked, called Mexican Stud. Stud deal, but every card is dealt down and you choose from your down cards which to roll up before each betting round. When I occasionally pulled trips to his two pairs, he'd shout through his beer, "Bring out the .32." Sure enough, a gun would appear. I lost two dollars. Pete wanted to know if I had anything stronger, "you know...that you smoke" because we "desert hicks want to try it." The next morning, my third at the trailhead, I followed a trail over a mountain shoulder to a hidden meadow noisy with wild turkey and grouse.

My fourth morning at the trailhead campground dawned clear and bright. The sun crossed the ridge at 8 a.m. After breakfast and sock washing, I hit the trail for Brainard Lake, four miles distant. The first mile wound through a lizard filled, desert flower arrayed arroyo to the base of a 9400-foot shoulder. Switch-backing up, I passed groundhogs, chipmunks, and grouse. Reaching higher elevation, the trail crossed some snow patches. Topping the ridge at last, the trail dipped down, passed Willow Lake, and then climbed again heading steadily toward the lofty crags of the Palisades. Brainard Lake appeared suddenly, tucked against a steep wall at the base of a heady tower. Just left of the lake stood a bald rock outcrop. Beyond, the view opened up, looking down and out for sixteen miles to the desert at Big Pine, and the arid White Mountains in the background. With clear sky above, a warm sun on my shoulders, and no one within miles, I shed my clothes and sunned in the breeze on the shore of the lake.

I returned to camp too late to pack up and leave. What to do in the morning? Return to Washington State, Snoqualmie

Charles A. Bookman | **The World Has Changed**

Pass to try to cut timber for Weyerhaeuser? If it's no go there, the Green Giant harvests peas in Dayton, Washington . They'll need operators for their pea-picking combine. If that's no go, then perhaps get rehired at Highlands Inn in Carmel before ending the summer with my friends in Wyoming's Teton mountains.

Back at the campground, I moved next to Lance and Peggy, the UCLA students who'd given me a ride up from the valley. Lance poured out his troubles: he'd been busted in California for "being in the vicinity" and in St. Petersburg, Florida, for selling to a cop ($1000 bail). California told him they'd fine him only $250 if he'd plead guilty and not contest the charge on grounds of illegal search and seizure, so he did. The Florida charge was headed to trial. In all probability, Florida meant jail, so he'd come to kiss Peggy, whom he'd met through work at The Resistance alternative newspaper, goodbye. They'd come to Big Pine Creek because Peggy had spent twelve summers in the area and thought it was beautiful. Her father, the head geologist at UCLA, had done his research there. He had used Big Pine as his base.

Gary Hepler, an experienced mountaineer who had picked me up hitchhiking a few days earlier, ambled over. Gary said that his crewcut didn't mean that he was a Navy man, although he had been in the Coast Guard. Gary and I decided to climb together since my people weren't showing and his climbing companions hadn't shown either. We chose as our destination Middle Palisade, a fourteener.

Next morning, following a full course breakfast at Glacier Lodge, where the owner described "his" route up the mountain, we set out, fully loaded with climbing gear, for Brainard Lake (again) and beyond. The mosquitos met us at Willow Lake. Soon after we reached what I had thought the day before was Brainard Lake, but Gary said it was too small to have a name. Brainard Lake turned out to be a glacial jewel another half hour further along the trail. We circled it from about 150 feet above, then bushwhacked on up to our base camp, Finger Lake, at 10,800 feet.

Long and narrow, Finger Lake resembles a fjord, with a shallow outlet and deep interior. The Middle Palisade glacier lies above. It must have cut the lake at some point, but has now receded. The lake was still largely covered with seasonal ice. But ice or no ice, after five miles of heavy packing, we took our boots off and bathed our feet. We made camp on a small tundra-like knoll. We turned in right after supper, acceding to the mountain reality that we stir out of the sack at 4:30 a.m.

Next morning, before dawn, we traversed the glacier. The angle and conditions were such that we didn't need crampons. Reaching the base of the peak at a steep gully, we climbed fourth and fifth class rock until we reached a 4-foot-wide ridge, with 1,000 feet of air on both sides. We followed the ridge up to the summit. Navy pilots spotted us and did dips and turns almost in our face. We waved. Going down, we stepped out on the glacier and glissaded down the bowl.

With dark approaching, we jogged the five miles back to our Big Pine camp with full backpacks. We were so winded when we reached the road, we couldn't talk.

It was time to move on. Gary gave me a ride down toward Lone Pine, California. I bivouacked that night in Alabama Hills, a giant basalt boulder field that has provided background for many a western movie. I decided to hitch around the southern end of the Sierras, then back up to Monterey. I caught rides along Highway 95 the next day toward Los Angeles. I needed a shower so sprang for a three-dollar-a-night motel in Kingsburg, California. The motel was sandwiched between the railroad tracks, the Del Monte packing house, and the freeway.

My rides the next day took me through fields of walnuts, figs, citrus, grapes, cotton, berries, fruits, and artichokes. Catching an extended ride with a mail carrier, I followed a circuitous route on logging roads in the western Sierra foothills. The mail carrier took me to the logging operations of Pine Logging and General Box companies. They weren't hiring, or at least they weren't hiring me. I spent the night at Dora Belle campground on Shaver Lake, northeast of Fresno.

Back at Highlands Inn

Returning to Carmel, I hired back at Highlands Inn. Instead of camping on the beach, I was offered a closet-sized room in the basement of the main lodge. The room turned out to be a disused bathroom where a piece of plywood over the tub served as the bed where I slept for ten days. Then, when one of the parking valets got fired for joy riding in a hotel guest's corvette, I moved across the basement hall into his room. I gained a little more space and also a roommate, the hotel's dishwasher, Francisco (Pancho) Perez Lemuz. Pancho told me about his family in Mexico when he was not watching his small black and white television. With his minimum wage earnings, he had paid for a modern house for his family in his native village. That's a lot of dishes, we both agreed.

One evening, I walked along Spindrift Drive, a coast-hugging lane just down the road from the Inn, it's where sea and rock meet. The architecture amplified the light and shadow of the coastline. Bold rectangles and other acute angles such as A-frames imitated sharp abutments of rock. Much of the outside woodwork was stained gray-brown, hues of kelp and the sea. One particular house rose on a rough granite knoll above the coast. The main house was a large rectangular box of gray-brown wood, with the upper seaward corner emphasized by the shadow of an indentation. The sea-facing walls were glass. Beside the main house stood an A-frame art studio painted orange-brown. Next to that was a smaller guest cottage. Below it all—far below—the surf pounded the rocks, spouting spume, froth, and bubbles.

Passing these special architectural statements, each more dramatic than the next, I mused about owning one. That one there, shaped like a horseshoe. No there, that Victorian gingerbread flanked by lavender beds. After a few minutes, I realized that owning one of those houses would deprive me of the dream of wanting to own one. I wrote at the time, "My spirit is nourished more by the *want* than the *own*. To want is to dream. To dream is to have the world. To own is to meet reality. To meet reality is to look back the way you've come rather than to focus on the future. I draw sustenance from the dream, the want, the yearning."

Only the dreamer can hobo, I thought. The dreamer can live free. The dreamer travels at will, preferably with a trade so that work is there when you need it. A prerequisite for dreaming is recognizing the boundaries of your dreaming. One needs to attend to realities. Dream of sleeping in a castle? Make sure you have a sleeping bag. One night your castle is a campfire, another night it's a piece of plywood balanced on an old bathtub. Help your mind translate your reality into your dreams, not the other way around. Fifty years later, I admire my youthful ruminations but I am not sure I still embrace them.

Summer's End

I left Highlands Inn at the end of July for the delayed rendezvous with my climbing buddies in the Grand Tetons. I caught good rides across California, Nevada, and Utah into Wyoming. One of my rides had just received a suspended sentence in California for selling marijuana. He faced similar charges in Colorado, and he was returning to stand trial. He knew he would not get off so lightly the second time around. "I've been selling all my life," he said. "There's nothing else I know, nothing else I want to know. I even sold to a cop. Now I'm up for sale and all sold out."

A different kind of salesman picked me up outside Rock Springs, Wyoming. "I came out from Detroit seven years ago with six *Speed Queen* vacuum cleaners in my trunk and $30 in my pocket. Last fall, I received an offer of $300,000 for my franchise. Can you sell boy, can you sell?" he asked. "Got to sell to get through this world in style."

My friends and I climbed for two weeks in the Tetons. A first ascent of a new route on Red Sentinel, a sub-summit of the Grand Teton, was a highlight. My climbing buddy Dave Ingalls described the route in *The American Alpine Journal*'s 1969 edition,

Charles A. Bookman | **The World Has Changed**

    The fourth route on this slender pinnacle was climbed July 27 by Dave Ingalls, Charles Bookman and Roy Kligfield. After the standard approach from the south, the overhanging inside corner on the southwest side was started by an F6 pitch to a cave. The next difficult lead began horizontally right via delicate balance from the cave. Hand traverses led to a vertical aid crack leading up to the dihedral. From a sling belay in the dihedral A3 nailing led onto an exposed face where unprotected F7 climbing took the party to the summit ridgelet.

    The next day, we climbed the Grand Teton. The route up was straightforward compared to the sketchy rock of the previous day. The highlight for me was the 120 foot airy rappel off the summit.

    One day, we drove over Teton Pass into Idaho to explore remote ice caves on the back side of the Teton Range. Wind Cave has a giant opening but narrows into a very tight passage. We explored with head lamps and climbing gear. Returning to the mouth of the cave after several hours underground, we were startled to find a mountain thunderstorm lodged above our valley. The highly local storm was generating lightning bolts at eye level. Taking advantage of a break in the storm, we jack-rabbited down the lengthy scree slope below the cave to the relative safety of the valley floor. Unfortunately, someone dislodged a rock that landed squarely on my hand. It was a good thing we had completed our major climbs, because my hand remained weak and useless for weeks.

    On Sundays, the ritzy Jenny Lake Resort held an all-you-can-eat brunch featuring fresh trout. The climbers' record for downing trout stood at sixteen. My buddy Dave Ingalls resolved to beat the record. We put on clean clothes for the occasion.

    I bore witness to Dave's performance. The first dozen trout were easy. Tying the record took Dave another half-hour. By then, the restaurant staff knew what was afoot—after all, many of them were climbers too.

    Dave was slowing down. I put trout 17 and 18 on his plate. He stared and stared, then took small, deliberate forkfuls until his plate was clean again. He sipped a little water. "You've broken the record," I said. "Do you want to call it a day?"

"Get me one more," Dave muttered. Dave stared at number 19. Number 19 stared back. After an agonizing fifteen minutes, he lifted his fork and number 19 slowly but steadily disappeared.

I think twenty trout had been Dave's goal, but he stopped at nineteen. I paid the bill while Dave slowly and deliberately left the table and plodded out of the dining room. I found him a few minutes later in the lobby bathroom where he had unburdened himself of many of those trout.

It was time to go home. We needed a car. There wasn't a lot of choice in the want ads. We purchased a 1953 Buick. The car had a broken exhaust system, which required driving with the windows open. Other than that, it seemed rugged enough to get us home. Not long after leaving Jackson, we stopped at a fireworks stand and loaded the trunk with fireworks, which would be illegal in New York, where we were headed. The fireworks remained in the trunk for months until one day, a New York state trooper opened the trunk—but that is another story.[1]

---

[1] See "Halloween Friends" in chapter 14 (page 195).

Chapter 8

Taxi Driver 1968—1970

Often when I am in a taxicab, I mention to the driver I used to drive a yellow cab in New York City. They warm immediately and if they hadn't already been talking, we immediately trade stories. When I worked at the Seattle Department of Transportation in the 2000s, I discovered that two of my colleagues also drove for hire in New York. One drove a black limo, the other a gypsy cab (gypsy cabs were telephone-based ride services similar to the app-based ride services of today). We enjoyed joshing gently about who had the most dangerous or difficult work. I have dined out on my taxi driving for more than fifty years.

Driving a yellow cab in New York City in the 1960s was one of the best times of my young life. I worked my own hours and the pay at twenty hours a week supported my student lifestyle. I talked up my driving and soon several friends also obtained hack licenses.

Passing the licensing exam in the municipal building on Worth Street was an achievement. In those days, you had to demonstrate extensive knowledge of the City—landmark locations, the best crosstown streets, and alternate routes to the airport. I studied as hard for that exam as I did for any test at Columbia University.

I drove for the Manhattanville yellow taxi garage at the west end of 125th Street. The evening shape-up began at 2 p.m. While I had my license and my union card, I never quite figured out that to get in and out quickly and to get a cab in good condition, you needed to slip the dispatcher three dollars. Being naïve or stubborn (I forget which, maybe both), often I sat for two hours while the other drivers got the good cabs. When the dispatcher finally gave me a cab, it was often one that had been in an accident and poorly repaired, with stiff erratic steering, no reverse gear, or dangerously compromised brakes. I bore it all with aplomb and always looked forward to my nighttime shift.

I drove for 10 to 12 hours, two or three nights a week. I started in rush hour. Later, I drove people home from restaurants or the theater. In the wee hours, the workers and the junkies needed rides. Everyone needs to get home.

Every night came with a story. I picked up a couple about 11:30 one Saturday night at the northeast corner of St. Marks Place and Third Avenue. They snuggled in the right corner of the back seat. His tie was as wide as his grin. He wore a crisp powder blue shirt. She sported a floppy hat and false eyelashes. Her mascara was slightly smeared. He asked to go to his place in Chelsea.

"Do you believe in astrology?" she asked him as I fought traffic on Third Avenue. "Are our signs compatible?"

"I'm a Pisces, that's a two-headed fish." He kissed her twice, once on each cheek. "What are you?"

"I'm a Scorpio, with stinging claws." She pinched him on the neck, hard. He yelped in pain, then hugged her closer.

Another evening, at the height of rush hour, I picked up a well-to-do-looking man at the corner of Columbus and 103rd Street. He asked to go to Penn Station. What was he doing in that neighborhood? I wondered, did he have a mistress? He got in the cab, and locked the door. Then within the privacy of his personal tin pan alley recording studio, he broke into a full basso rotundo. My rush hour Don Giovanni rattled the plastic partition with his low notes. "Say Don," I said, "Want me to drive you to the Met?"

"Get me to the train on time." Ok. Ok.

One Wednesday night, I drove a bowler-hatted man and his chalk-faced companion, dressed in a white evening gown, to a banquet at the Waldorf Astoria Hotel. At least the gown had been white. It was wintertime, freezing rain, and she had stepped in deep slush.

The freezing rain along Park Avenue made driving difficult. My wipers left muddy streaks. I sped up where I could and braked hard sometimes to ease the jolt from the potholes or to stop at a light.

"Sonny," the woman rapped on the barrier. "Your braking is giving me whiplash."

Whiplash or no, I figured this couple was good for only a 25 cent tip.

A young mother with two kids hailed me one afternoon on Park Avenue in the upper '80s. She was ferrying her children from the doctor's office to their home at East 79th Street and East End Avenue. The girl was old enough to read, and the boy was

Coming of Age Stories

missing a couple of teeth. The doctor had given them lollipops, and they were wiggly from the sugar. Standing up on the seat, the girl leaned forward to read my name on the plastic photo identification card in the dusty bracket to the right of the meter.

"His name is Charlie," she said.

"Charlie?" repeated the boy. "Good and plenty Charlie?"

Together they sang as I made my turn onto 79th Street—"Oweee, good and plenty good and plenty good and plenty Charlie good and plenty good and plenty good and plenty plenty good Charlie—Non-stop for six rush hour crosstown blocks. Arriving at their destination the kids zoomed out of the car. "Aren't they cute?" the mother chirped. "How much do I owe you?"

"That's alright," I said. "This one's on me."

The taxi business slows between 8:30 and 10:30 p.m. Workers are home and the restaurants and theaters are packed with patrons who aren't yet ready to leave. I spent these hours cruising the midtown hotels. I often picked up a tourist looking for entertainment or action. One night, I picked up a well-dressed man with an Afro outside the Plaza Hotel. "What is there to do in this town?" he asked.

"What are you up for?" I replied.

"Minority recruitment. In town from Richmond, Virginia. Can you find me a big city woman? It's lonely up there on the ninth floor."

"State your preference. Own kind? Big money? Hot time or you like cooling it over a few drinks in a jazz house?"

"This is the big city, brother, can you show it to me?"

"Listen my Richmond friend, my world is largely white and you ask me about the other side of the tracks. I can ferry you up to Lenox Avenue and let you off on a corner but you'll lose your billfold faster than your barber cuts your hair or I can cruise slowly through midtown until you find someone on the street corner who is looking for company.

"This'll do," he said. He had seen what he wanted. He hopped out on the corner of 7th Avenue and 53rd Street, in front of the Americana Hotel. As I reset my meter and updated my time sheet, I watched him sidle up to a six-foot-tall street walker. With her big wig and garish lips, she looked like she could take on the seven dwarfs all at once. She lit a cigarette as they discussed services and price.

Virginia seemed to have a lock on visitors looking for a good time in the big city. I picked up a couple of guys from Virginia on 79th Street outside Mike Malkan's pub. One of them carried a fifth in his coat pocket.

They yucked it up in the back seat. Finally, I asked them, "Where to?"

"Take us to the gulls."

"Huh? Staten Island Ferry? 125th Street pier?"

"Isn't that how you say it in the big city? Goils. You know."

"You have a difficult choice, gentlemen, " I said as I turned right onto Second Avenue. "Note the many establishments. The bar on your left attracts executive secretaries. Across the street, down the block, you will find intermediate-school teachers. Malachy's beckoning in the next block pulls them in from the outer boroughs."

I turned right on 57th Street, then right again on 3rd Avenue. "Now this, my friends is a higher class avenue. Most have dates, at least chaperones, though this should not deter the forward among you."

"Jeez, I can't decide," one guy said.

"Third Avenue is also noted for its high class dirty movies and the headquarters of the FBI on 70th Street. Mafia boss Joe Colombo once picketed there for Italian decency. Every high rise you pass is chockablock with airline stewardesses sharing apartments, secretaries yearning for a college man."

I turned back down 79th Street, and again on 2nd Avenue, the meter was close to two dollars now and they were still undecided.

"Where are we?" they asked.

One of the finest neighborhoods on the island, my friends. Reserved for the well-heeled."

"It's getting late," one of them said, somewhat sobered up. "We thought you could help us."

Coming of Age Stories

"I shall drop you at the hub of the night world, the Americana Hotel, at 7th Avenue and 53rd Street. You will have your choice of street walkers there."

"Why, that's where we're staying."

The fare, $3.25; the tip $1.75.

I picked up a lot of fares in the vicinity of the Americana Hotel. Four businessmen hopped in one evening. The guy in the passenger seat next to me had a brassy voice and a bulgy midriff. Disdainfully extending a bill my way, he says, "Here's one for the road and there's more where that came from. Take us to the Cattle Baron Restaurant. We'd like a real New York cut."

Maybe I was in a bad mood that day. "Well, you're getting a real New York cut," I said. "Please get out of my cab, now. Go find another hack." They protested, took my number. But I kept their dollar bill. I was trying to teach them a lesson in manners.

An odd trio of young men hailed me in Times Square. One wore a cast on his arm, obviously fake. "Take us to Coney Island," he said.

I pulled up to the curb, turned around, looked directly at them and said, "You've got to be kidding." I didn't budge. They squirmed.

"Come on," the spokesman whined. I didn't budge. After another long minute, they opened the door and left my cab. "Go rob somebody else," I mused.

I always enjoyed taking working people home late at night. These were typically long, late night runs to the outer boroughs. With good fares came good tips, especially since working people appreciated that a cabbie would actually take them to the South Bronx or East Brooklyn.

Sometimes, these long rides would involve suspicious people or dodgy neighborhoods. Returning to midtown from the Bronx, my final fare one night was an off-duty detective wanting a ride home to Harlem. I figured I could drop him at his apartment and then it would be a short home run over to my garage. It must have been about 3 a.m. Suddenly, my passenger snorted. "Junk!" he cried. "I smell junk in this cab. Who you been driving?"

I explained I had just driven a woman, possibly strung out, home to the Bronx. "I didn't know junk smelled," I said.

"I smell it everywhere," he said. "Rough city, tough job. No matter." He dozed off and I delivered him safely to his apartment.

In midtown at the height of rush hour, my new passenger rapped with his umbrella on the glass. "LaGuardia. Will I make my plane?"

"Where you flying to?"

"District of Columbia."

"In this traffic, we'll never make it." Seven minutes already and we had crawled just one block.

"You could have walked to the Pan Am Building and taken a helicopter. Or taken the train. No, of course, we'll never make it. No problem, though. There's always a later plane."

Who expects a smooth ride from Sixth Avenue and 43rd Street to LaGuardia Airport at 5:30 in the afternoon? I got him to the airport in 46 minutes and he made his flight. How did I do this? By circumnavigating Manhattan Island. I took the FDR Drive south around the Battery to the West Side Highway (the West Side Highway didn't collapse until 1973). We passed the derelict liner piers, 79th street boat basin, and the tennis courts in Riverside Park. Continuing north, we drove past the 125th Street sanitation pier, through neighborhoods of broken glass and shattered dreams, to Robert Moses' Cross Bronx Expressway, where we mingled with New Jersey traffic for a moment. Then down the Harlem River Drive, always lightly trafficked—it's as though no one knows it's there, maybe because it doesn't go anywhere. Who wants to go from Dyckman Street to Pleasant Avenue? From there, we debouched onto the Triborough Bridge, and right to LaGuardia.

The longest distance, shortest time. I always made it on time in the greatest city in the world.

Chapter 9

Whitehall Street
1969—1970

It is hard to understand now, the pressure that the war exerted on us young men to stay in college. I wanted nothing more at that time than my freedom, to roam the country and the planet, to experience the land and the people and to find out who I was.

The reality was that a brief lapse, a momentary pause, in my academic record and I would become cannon fodder for President Lyndon Johnson's war. The idea intrigued me when I was a freshman in 1966. The Tet Offensive hadn't happened yet. The war was still far away. By 1968, the time of Columbia University's spring uprising in 1968, the danger and the carnage of the war dominated the evening television news. Academic deferments were on the way out, to be replaced by a lottery system. Some would be lucky and draw a high number in the lottery, unlikely to be called up.

Charles A. Bookman | The World Has Changed

Everyone I knew tried to figure out a path to escape the noose. My roommate, Jack Yatteau already tall and skinny, spent the fall of 1969 subsisting on grapefruit and eggs, trying to get leaner and leaner until his body mass index (BMI) would fall below U.S. Army standards. If you tried that, sometimes the Selective Service System would remand you to a dormitory and feed you normally for two weeks and then retest you. Jack was lucky. He stayed below the required BMI.

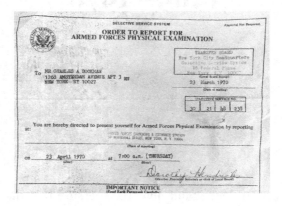

For reasons that mystify me to this day, I studied overtime to shorten my academic career. I took classes for part of the summer of 1969, then loaded up with 19 credits in the fall semester, to complete my academic tenure at Columbia in three and a half years, instead of the requisite four. At last, as of December, 1969, I would be out from under schooling!

The first Selective Service lottery took place that same month. I drew number 195, the highest number to be called in my district. My letter to report to the Whitehall Street Induction Center came just after the first of the year. Arlo Guthrie summed up the Whitehall physical experience pretty well in his legendary song *Alice's Restaurant* (1967):

Coming of Age Stories

>They got a building down New York City, it's called Whitehall Street,
>Where you walk in, you get injected, inspected, detected, infected,
>Neglected and selected. I went down to get my physical examination one
>Day, and I walked in, I sat down, got good and drunk the night before, so
>I looked and felt my best when I went in that morning. 'Cause I wanted to
>Look like the all–American kid from New York City, man I wanted, I wanted
>To feel like the all–, I wanted to be the all American kid from New York,
>And I walked in, sat down, I was hung down, brung down, hung up, and all
>Kinds o' mean nasty ugly things. And I walked in and sat down and they gave
>Me a piece of paper, said, "Kid, see the psychiatrist, room 604."

No room 604 for me. I stripped to my skivvies with the rest of the recruits and filed from test to test—height, weight, eyesight, hernia check (look left and cough). At each station, you received a slip of paper, which you tucked into a manila envelope. After a morning of poking and prodding, the envelope bulged with the test slips. Then you waited.

Finally, you were called with your envelope to the evaluation room, where the assignment clerks filled one side of a long table and the recruits stood along the other side. My clerk asked for my folder. I handed the folder over. He carefully opened the clip and removed the contents. He organized them right-side up and started to transfer their results to a standard GI form. Then he paused.

He looked over his shoulder, first to the right, then to the left. Then, looking directly at me, he leaned across the table and whispered, "You don't want to join the Army, do you?" I said, "No sir."

Charles A. Bookman | **The World Has Changed**

He finished his form. I was directed to dress and told that I would hear from my draft board within a few weeks.

I never heard from my draft board again. Whether my paperwork became lost, or I had some disqualifying condition, I would never know. I certainly didn't inquire. In those pre-computer days, perhaps direct action was a little bit easier. I figure the corporal clerk was engaged in his own private anti-war effort and I was the beneficiary.

My brief visit to Whitehall Street would have been in January 1970. In March, I left with Arno Vosk and Richard Stern to watch a solar eclipse in Norfolk, VA and then to climb the big Mexican volcanoes. Right after that, I joined the scientific crew of the *R/V Conrad*, signing on in Acapulco and leaving the ship eight months later in Cape Town, South Africa. If my draft board had wanted me, they would have had a devil of a time catching up with me.

Chapter 10

Plate Tectonics
1970—1973

After I left college, I spent three years working as a seagoing electronics technician on oceanographic ships. I worked in the South Pacific and South Atlantic Oceans, and the Mediterranean Sea. The data I gathered on seafloor temperatures helped confirm the theory of plate tectonics, which was radical then and is today accepted science. I reached a point in my oceanographic career where it was "learn math and get a PhD" or move on. I moved on to graduate school at the University of Rhode Island (URI), where I earned a policy degree in marine affairs. My classmates at URI were largely mid-career uniformed U.S. Navy and Coast Guard personnel. They were my first exposure to public service. I was impressed with their dedication and drive, and I have never looked back on my career choices.

Charles A. Bookman | **The World Has Changed**

1970, Acapulco, Mexico to Cape Town, South Africa on *R/V Conrad*

My shipmates came from around the world. The Bos'n, John Santini's torso was covered with tattoos. Alex Gonsalves, the cook had a family in Goa who he hadn't seen in three years. Luis Soto, our able electronics technician hailed from Argentina. George Conrad, the deep sea photographer had previously owned a small postcard photography business in Digby, Nova Scotia. Ivo Gregor, my watchmate and sometime roommate, had been a telegrapher in the Czech Army. He kept his coding sharp by keying in articles from old *Time* magazines. Our floating United Nations was completely cut off from girlfriends, family, and home. News arrived by shortwave radio ("This is Radio Cuba..."). The typical voyage ran for a month; the longest nearly six weeks. Port calls for refueling, resupply and recreation lasted up to four days, except in Cape Town, where we had six weeks of shore liberty while the ship was overhauled.

I became totally engrossed in my work. My notes from the time include extensive descriptions of shipboard life and science, and accounts of adventures at sea and in exotic ports of call.

R/V Conrad

The R/V Conrad was equipped by the Navy with a prototype global positioning (GPS) system called SatNav. Motorola operated the satellite system, including the receivers. The data were processed using an early minicomputer called the DEC PDP 8, which had the computing power of an early Commodore 64. When the system worked, it provided accurate real-time positioning anywhere on the globe. More often than not, however, some electronic component would fail midway through the month-long leg at sea. When the inevitable happened, we would rely on LORAN or sextant (depending where in the world we were). If technicians from Motorola and DEC were not onboard, they would meet the ship at our infrequent port calls.

Late in 1970, the R/V *Conrad* completed a thirty-one day leg from Abidjan, Ivory Coast, to Moçâmedes, Angola, and then a thirty-five day leg from Moçâmedes along the Walvis Ridge and deep into the "roaring forties" to an extended port call in Cape Town, South Africa. (Today's rich oil fields off Nigeria, Congo, and Angola were originally confirmed by our early geophysical mapping of the region.) The satellite navigation equipment went out somewhere and Moçâmedes was so remote that the traveling technicians didn't show up, so we completed the roaring forties leg without the help of the prototype GPS. With thirty- to forty-foot waves rolling ceaselessly under the keel, bracing yourself against the taffrail felt like surfing. The sky was gray, we didn't see the sun for weeks. One evening in the mess, I asked our captain, Alan Jorgensen, where we were. He replied in his usual droll style, "somewhere east of Kansas."

East Pacific, April, 1970. I joined the ship in Acapulco, Mexico. There she was, riding at anchor at a dock close to the center of the port. My shipmates were busy with their shore time. Several of us escorted three divorcees, all receptionists for a Holiday Inn in East Lansing, Michigan—names Marcy, Darcy, and Sandra—to the dirtiest of all Mexican bordellos, Las Huarache. The place was famous. Veiled floozies walked up to you, shook you by the short arm, giggled, poked, pecked, tickled, and teased. There was nothing like it in East Lansing, and Marcy, Darcy, and Sandra couldn't get enough of the scene.

Charles A. Bookman | **The World Has Changed**

I took one of the women to my favorite local beach, Pie de la Cuesta, about eight miles out of town. We drank rum and cokes and ate shrimp grilled over charcoal under a palapa while we watched fins break the surf. I thought they were sharks, but the mamacita at the grill told us they were rays.

At sea, we didn't spy many other vessels, except when crossing the shipping lane for the Panama Canal. Riding the gentle swells, the water was as warm as ninety-four degrees. We saw sharks and squid and sunsets every day. Now and then a sea turtle lazed by, or a pod of porpoises. Sometimes large rolling waves passed under the keel. Other times the sea lay flat and heavy, like plate glass. When it did that before noon, heavy yet placid swells followed in early evening, and lightning punctuated the night sky. One night our radio antennas glowed with pale blue Saint Elmo's fire.

The sharks complicated our daily swim stations, where we would swan dive off the vessel. Like dolphins, we sliced through the water for a minute or so. These dips were hasty because, there were things in the water, and we could see them. As a shipmate prepared to dive off the bridge, he would ask the lookout if there's anything below, get a belated nod, then spring. Arching in mid-flight he might hear a belated "Uhh, wait a minute, there's a shark on the port side." Arms would thrash mid-dive as he tried to climb up from whence he came. His dive would become a mad belly flop, followed swiftly by a veritable aquatic leap to the boat, a mad scramble to the security of the ship.

In a moment of calm, paddling twenty or thirty yards off the boat, I would turn. My ship floated alone, unhurried, rocking in the gentle swell. How small my shipboard world was compared to the vast ocean. I kicked bicycle fashion to keep afloat. I felt like I could paddle to China and back but knew intuitively it was time to swim back to the ship, back to my world.

Work on an oceanographic research ship was all-consuming. The schedule ran on a twenty-four-hour clock. There was never a day off. Sleep was a rare quantity as a working ship was a noisy ship. No one thought of anything else besides work. If

Coming of Age Stories

you did, you became frustrated because you didn't have access to other outlets. I wrote about these first weeks at sea:

> My technician's skills are laughable at best, but this hasn't proved a great handicap, and I don't think I'm in danger of being fired, though if I remain as poor a technician as I was at the beginning (neatness and accuracy have never been part of my skill set), I don't expect to stay on long. Good data should start rolling in soon. I am an eternal optimist. Let's hope my employers are, too.
>
> I stand watch in the "dry lab" in four-hour shifts twice a day, for a total of eight hours. Our instruments record our progress in continuous data streams. There's the precision depth recorder (a form of sonar), and the magnetometer, also a read-out for the gravimeter and for the ship's speed, direction, and heading. There's a work bench for me and the photographer, and our darkroom is nearby as well. Almost every day, the ship stops one or more times for a "station," where we lower seabed coring instruments to the seabed. The process takes about three hours depending on the water depth. Then there's the time I spend maintaining and repairing my equipment. Add it all together, the workday extends to sixteen hours. If you are not sleeping or eating, you are working or at least discussing or thinking about work.

Strapping the thermograd onto the deepsea coring apparatus

Charles A. Bookman | **The World Has Changed**

I am directly responsible for the thermograd ("Tgrad," we call it), sort of a rectal thermometer for the earth. Thermal probes attached to the deep sea core measure the flow of heat from the earth. The theory is that the closer the core is taken to centers of thermal upwelling, like mid-ocean ridges, the more active the heat flow.

I'm not holding on to the 1,500-pound core head as it plunges into the deep, I'm on deck, watching the core wire spin off the large drum, ready to process data and make repairs when my instrument resurfaces. My work meshes with at least five other shipboard jobs. I must operate my machine as efficiently as possible on other people's equipment—the deep sea coring machine, and the photographic lab. This calls for diplomacy and tact, skill, intuition, and a foul mouth in the best sailor tradition. First, I load the Tgrad in the darkroom, camera operator shoved aside. Next, separate components of the Tgrad—its external sensors, the heavy recording-equipment housing, and the wires connecting the sensors with the recorder—have to be strapped to the coring pipe, with the entire coring crew (three people) buzzing around badmouthing my sweet machine. The Tgrad is blamed for every bent pipe pulled up off the seafloor. The competition, me trying to get their pipes bent and them trying to bust my probes to smithereens, is intense. Finally, certain portions of my data must be gathered in the coring lab. The core describer, a very pushy Ohioan, reluctantly lets me enter to make my measurement and then summarily ushers me out. Institutionally, the Tgrad man takes a lot of guff and gives it. It's a role that has to be played, and that part of the job at least I do very well.

Neatness and painstaking exactitude are the hallmarks of good data gathering. These are not my strengths, but I am learning every day and beginning to harvest good data.

We run seismic lines up and down the flanks of the Galapagos Islands in the cool Peru Current (also called the Humboldt Current). Rafts of squid are attracted to our powerful floodlights during nighttime coring stations. Just beyond the squid, we make out waves of sea turtles feeding on them. Big giant shelled sea critters, all green and barnacle encrusted. Dolphins, sea birds and sharks are everywhere. Mornings, the ship's decks are covered with blue-bodied, gossamer-winged flying fish.

Coming of Age Stories

Panama, May 1970. The Canal Zone was a very strange place. One side of the street was Panama City, where all the important buildings were protected by chain link fences and armed guards equipped with automatic rifles and tear gas grenades. The other side of the street was a 1948 U.S. army company town. The war was over, the economy was booming. The word imperialism still meant good times. Split level houses, electricity, suburbs, greenery. The breeze smelled of jungle. Company movie houses, company diners, company dry goods stores, no bars. I asked for fishing tackle for sharks at the company hardware store. A sweet clerk named Irma told me that she couldn't sell to me unless I had a Panama Canal Company card. Earlier, a Canal Zone police officer had said "Howdy." I asked Irma if I could purchase my shark tackle through an employee. She said speak to the manager. The manager said, "Just don't let me know about it." So, I asked around. People started to give lip, "That's against the law."

"Oh, I wouldn't do that, this is a company store."

"Oh my. I might lose my job."

Total purchase price would have been $2.46.

The people who lived in the zone ran a fine canal. The massive locks operated like elevators, with water doing the heavy lifting. Jungle pressed in on the reaches between the locks. We listened to monkeys chatter while sipping Coca-Cola on the fantail. Portions of the waterway reminded me of the Okefenokee Swamp. We even spotted alligators.

The Run to Cartagena, Colombia. The chief scientist wanted some data from the continental shelf, so we ran seismic lines up, down, and along the shallow coast of Panama's roadless Darien Peninsula. I had researched this area in college, as I reviewed alternative routes for a new canal. With the aid of our excellent hydrographic maps, I was able to pick out the proposed routes that I had researched and discussed. This kind of data was thrilling stuff for me as I compared reliefs and profiles. What luck, three days immersed in legendary geography. A better voyage leg than I could have wished for. The only thing more enticing for me would have been to cross the peninsula on foot, encountering its native people and other lawless inhabitants. That would have to wait for another time.[1]

A Month in the Caribbean. My impression of the Caribbean was always that of a flat-lying, idyllically blue tropical sea. The reality really hit the fantail. Thirty-foot swells were common after we left Cartagena, Colombia. The trade winds made for scudding weather, with their breezes blowing steadily at twenty knots. A bigger blow and a rain squall would pass over us every few days, then the winds would reach near gale force. Our ship rocked and rolled through the Caribbean.

The lively sea made for beautiful scenery; the bow cutting through gigantic swells that towered menacingly over the vessel, the decks awash with spray, walls of green water breaking over the rails. With the ship pitching at odd angles, interesting happenings occurred on board. Your chair would suddenly lurch of its own accord, spilling you across the floor. Any equipment not tied down landed on the floor. The camera operator, in the first few days of this leg, was stubborn about tying his gear. His delicate undersea cameras smashed to the floor five times before he finally learned. Once an empty chair picked itself up and hurtled five feet through space to crash into a computer used to calculate gravity anomalies. That put the expensive equipment out of commission until it could be repaired.

And try to sleep through this ruckus! I awoke once with an electric fan whirring in my bed. That same night the overhead fluorescent light fixture clattered from the ceiling to the floor. My alarm clock that morning was the sound of my head smashing against the sink—a hollow bonk—when I was thrown out of bed.

---

[1] Two years later, driving the Pan American Highway with my girlfriend, we drove to the literal end of the road. We shipped our car across the Darien Gap, and we passed through the canal (again) on an Italian steamship. That story is in chapter 12.

Coming of Age Stories

Hanging over the side of the vessel to attach my probes to the core pipe, walls of water crashed over me. I felt like I was surfing, holding my position, hanging ten. Wet clothes were a constant. Fortunately, the temperatures in the Caribbean were so mild, the fewer clothes the better.

Getting used to rough seas took a little something out of us. When we left Cartagena, we embarked on a cooperative program with the Colombian government. Two guest researchers joined us. One was the chair of the Department of Geology at the National University at Bogota, the other the dean of the School of Science. The dean served collaterally in the government and was in line to join the cabinet. Half an hour out of Cartagena, hitting our first rough seas, they both leaned over the rail, their faces thoroughly white. Their situation never improved. Not that they were alone in those first days in the Caribbean. Many of us joined them at one time or another. But after three days we were eating hearty again while the Colombians still subsisted on saltine crackers. When not on deck gazing vacantly at the horizon or leaning over the rail, they sat on a couch in the drafting room with their eyes shut tight. Every two hours or so they clambered out to the rail to clear their system. Then back to the couch.

The geology department chair was my roommate, and on those rare occasions when he had the courage to enter the room he'd drape himself over his leather suitcase in the top bunk and groan. He didn't unpack. Nor did he remove the suitcase from his bed before lying on it. After five days both men asked to be let off. We pulled into Santa Marta, Colombia, a seaside resort, just long enough to meet the customs boat and wave goodbye to our scientific partners. They were so weak by this time they could hardly walk, and the geology professor couldn't carry his suitcase. I never heard, but I wonder what the repercussions were for our partnership with the Colombians of their premature departure.

We spent a month in this fabled part of the world, running seismic lines up and down the Windward Isles—Guadeloupe, Dominica, Saint Lucia, Saint Vincent, Barbados, and Martinique.

Charles A. Bookman | **The World Has Changed**

People paid good money for scenic voyages such as this, cruising in the sweet sunlight from island to island.

Our Caribbean idyll wrapped up with a port call in Trinidad. Like every good sailor, I craved a cold beer. Trinidad is British and Guinness Stout is standard fare. My search for a beer led to an improbable encounter. With Georges di Georgio, our resident Chilean-Tahitian-Italian-Mexican who had been everywhere and done everything and if he hadn't, he said he had, I went wharf-side and imbibed a copious quantity of stout. Georges could barely walk, and I wanted to crawl. Mr. Prince our taxi driver picked us up in his '54 Caddy with twin klaxon horns mounted in front.

Once seated, Georges leaned over to the driver and said, "take us to the girls." Mr. Prince drove up to a Roman Catholic church. We looked at each other, and then at Mr. Prince, who said, "This is the place, man."

We thanked him, hopped out, and stumbled into the slat-wood building. Inside, people were on their knees, the women with headscarves. We stumbled about the rear pews asking for the bartender, and wondering just what was going on. I asked Georges if he really thought this was the place and as he answered, a loud "Amen" arose from up front. Georges, catching himself, said loudly, "Of course it is, hear? They've just caught sight of us."

Then, turning to the priest, he shouted, "Two stouts, man!" Before the priest could call down some kind of wrath on our innocent heads, and before I could drag Georges out of there, he walked right down front. Tugging on the monsignor's robes, Georges asked him for two young ones. I dashed out, not waiting for lightning to split the old roof. I ran right back to Mr. Prince who was wetting his pants with laughter and pointing to a dimly lit building across the street with a Coca-Cola sign out front.

Our three days in Port of Spain were punctuated with frequent heavy downpours. Eager for an on-land adventure and to try out the road bike I had just purchased from Georges, I set out—despite the rain—to camp on Trinidad's wild north shore.

Coming of Age Stories

My brief jungle idyll took a few unexpected turns and ended up being a night to remember.[1]

I planned to pedal over a two-thousand-foot jungle pass then down to the sea where, hopefully, I would find a quiet cove for camping. After sixteen miles over the pass, puffing and panting through rain showers, I descended to the seaside. It was late afternoon, and the only sign of habitation was a shack high above the road. The woman at the shack was shooing her pigs into the pen for the night. She said she would be glad to cook me a meal. I dined handsomely on fresh killed chicken, scrawny but delicious, with potatoes and native greens.

Leaving her hospitality behind, I pedaled a few more miles along the shore road and found my corner of rainforest just before pitch-dark. I made camp in a lovely glade under xerophyte-draped trees. Insects were a nuisance, but the lightning bugs lit up the dark like arc lamps. They say that the jungle never sleeps. It's also true that it's hard to sleep in the jungle with all the animal calls, insect buzzes, and chirps.

I dozed off. Then the rain returned. Even under my gigantic tree I was getting wet. The arc lamp fireflies held my attention. I had no idea what the other background noises were from, but I imagined all manner of other creatures. I closed my eyes and dreamed of the squirrels and pigeons in Central Park in New York. I asked them politely to quiet down. I forgot my peanuts. Damn. Reality intruded. A large bat swooped down among the rain and the insects. I poked my head out of my mummy bag. Eyes. Lots of eyes in my flashlight beam. Bats? Monkeys?

A trusty handbook titled, "*How to Survive in the Woods* says to address wild animals in a firm, soft reassuring tone. But I was feeling defenseless with all the eyes. I had had enough. Slowly, so as not to disturb the monkeys or bats or whatever the eyes belonged to, I picked up my gear, shook off the jungle

---

[1] Georges had bought the bike from a retired French Tour de France racer who had brought it with him to Tahiti. After having a heart attack on it, the racer sold it to Georges.

slime and millipedes and returned in the dark to my bicycle. Through jungle rain and fog, I retraced my sixteen miles, this time at night, in the rain. I moved slowly, walking and feeling my way when visibility was nil. The lights of Port of Spain were a welcome sight.

Crossing the Atlantic, Summer 1970. About halfway between America and Africa, we crossed the equator. We moved at the same pace as the stormy petrels that flanked us. At least that's what John Santini, the mate, said they were.

John Santini, Bos'n, R/V Conrad

I spent nearly a year at sea with Santini, the *R/V Conrad*'s bos'n. He was from the great Santini family of New York, which owned a very successful moving company called the Seven Santini Brothers. He was the eighth Santini brother, he liked to say. He dropped out of Massachusetts Institute of Technology in the early sixties, became a bos'n, and hadn't set foot on land—literally—for nearly four years.

Coming of Age Stories

I have a picture of Santini taken somewhere in the South Atlantic. He sits bare-chested on the fantail of the *Conrad*, looking into the camera. He holds an albatross, which he has carved. The bollard in front of him is covered with carving tools. The bird is very graceful. His shirt is off, revealing his many tattoos. A square-rigger with full sail rides the bounding main of his chest. A peacock covers his right breast, a parrot his left. Seagulls fly above each armpit. His right arm is covered from top to bottom by a pirate, another ship, Popeye the sailor man eating spinach, a shark, and assorted other fish and fowl. The left arm is hard to make out. I think I see a sea monster, a palm tree, and another pirate ship.

Santini was a gentle and interesting man. He could discuss Sartre or the tattoo parlors of Manila with equal ease. He showed a generation of would-be sailors how to chip paint and never lost his cool. He gave me a copy of *Papillon*, the true-to-life novel about an escape from France's Devil's Island penal colony, to read in the original French. I admired him greatly, a workingman's philosopher, salt of the sea.

We were hardly alone, even in the middle of nowhere. Three hundred-fifty miles from land we came across an abandoned fishing boat, shipshape, just no one on board. Signs of a meal cooked, then abandoned, a distress flag rigged of torn clothing; a man's watch, a hat, and a mariner's compass—no seafarer leaves his compass behind. The seas had been rough all month long. Had the fisherman fallen overboard? We radioed the U.S. Coast Guard in Miami. They knew about the boat. It had been abandoned two days before in rough seas.

Another evening I was just going off watch when someone sighted a distress beacon on the horizon. Racing to the scene, we found a large shrimp boat, the *Western 6*, adrift with a broken motor and a leak. Its crew was pumping water out using a gasoline-powered pump with but two gallons of fuel left. Water was coming in faster than it was being pumped out. They had been fighting the leak for five days. Another boat from their fleet, *Western 4*, was in the vicinity trying to find them but since they didn't know where the other boat was, they weren't having much luck. We established their position and made radio contact with *Western 4*. When *Western 4* finally hove into view, we steamed off.

Four hundred miles off the South American coast, the center of our social life is the two thousand dollar short-wave radio that pulls in Radio Guyana and Radio Surinam. Radio Guyana featured a weekly amateur hour. Among other things, we enjoyed *Nearer my God to Thee* played on a bamboo flute and *Red Sails in the Sunset* hummed on a wax paper-covered comb. Radio Guyana faded as we crossed the Atlantic and soon we were enraptured by Radio Senegal, with its captivating Afro-beat. The Voice of America reached us almost everywhere, but it insisted on broadcasting episodes in the life of Thomas Jefferson, while Radio Cuba featured soul thumping folk singers. I memorized the words to *Guantanamera*. The BBC World Service relied heavily on dry discussion of why Britain lost the Suez Canal, delivered by junior faculty members at the London School of Economics.

Reading took a turn for the worse as books not yet read became scarcer. Increasingly desperate, I boned up on the complete life history of South America's only species of edible frog, *Leptodactylus pentadactylus*, the South American Smoky Jungle Frog. Others on board became experts on Serbo-Croatian history, and the twenty-four works of the Tarzan series, by Edgar Rice Burroughs.

Our toothpaste came from Mexico, soy sauce from New Zealand (China Lily Brand). The peanut butter from New South Wales, Australia is labeled as peanut paste.

We are here for science. Thanks to *New York Times* science reporter Walter Sullivan's interest in the emerging field of plate tectonics, we are much closer to the pages of the *New York Times* than one might believe. The *Times* covers the exploits of the *Glomar Challenger*, an oceanographic vessel that has just accomplished the feat of drilling a hole 20,000 feet deep in the ocean floor. Until just a few months ago, this had never been done, and the *Glomar Challenger*, the only ship equipped for such work, was slated to drill more holes to confirm the theory of plate tec-

Coming of Age Stories

tonics. We could be considered the advance team because we were surveying future drilling sites, crisscrossing the sites to assemble detailed maps, and underlying seismic and geophysical data to help plan future drilling.

Life on board worked on twelve hour cycles. At 7:30 a.m., I was woken up by the preceding watch, with just enough time to get dressed and eat breakfast before reporting to the dry lab. For the next four hours three of us would tend data recorders that chart ocean depths, sub-ocean sediment layers, ocean gravity, and geomagnetism. Standing watch involved changing recording paper, replenishing ink supplies, making necessary repairs and in general ensuring that good data was gathered. Problems that arose ranged from short circuits and electrical fires to "acts of God." For example: towed behind the ship was an air gun, like a gigantic pop gun, that was used as a source for bouncing sound waves off the sea floor. At about 7:58 one morning a shark bit into the air hoses that fed compressed air to the gun. Repairing the hoses involved hauling in the gear and drying it; then, repairing and taping over the toothmarks. After the repair has cured, the air hose would be tested and if it passed inspection, restreamed so that data collection could be resumed. The repair took a couple of hours, which would show up in the trip report as a gap in the seismic data..

The next watch arrived at noon. After a short lunch, I would try to sleep until supper unless there was work to do. At least once a day the ship stopped for a station, in which instruments were lowered to the sea floor. My instrument, which measured temperatures of subsea sediments would be strapped to the forty-foot-long subsea coring device. I needed to be ready for those hours when the ship was on station. From the time the boat slowed, and we hauled in the scientific gear that streamed behind the ship, to the time we made way again, four hours elapsed. The ship could go on station any hour of day or night. Station took priority over all other activities—watch standing, eating, sleeping.

On an ideal day, the ship stopped for a station in the middle of the afternoon instead of the middle of the night, so the sta-

Charles A. Bookman | **The World Has Changed**

tion was over in time for supper. After supper on this ideal day, I would sleep or write a letter, maybe lose money at poker. Then the cycle would be repeated. Two four-hour watches a day; four-hour ship stations occurring at any time of day or night.

The dry lab was the social center of the ship. Since that was where the watch-standing took place, someone was always there to talk with. The short wave radio was there, and magazines littered the floor.

A ship is a noisy place with its massive diesel engines. Oceanography adds its own noises as well. Each data recorder has its own peculiar tick or ping. Towed behind the ship, the air gun fired every few seconds with a throaty "whump." Its sound waves bounced off the ocean floor with their own audible echoes.

Other noises kicked in when we stopped for a station. The hydraulic winch for the seafloor tripod cameras whined. The diesel winch that lowers the 2,000-pound seafloor coring device grumbled and cleared its throat and grumbled some more for two long, noisy hours. Out of all the scientific noises the most pleasant noise on board came out of my little instrument, the Tgrad. It rode silently down to the seabed, strapped to the outside of the core pipe. When turned on, the spooling optical data recording film inside purred soft and throaty, more like a pleased cat than clunky machinery.

The goal of all those noises was to understand the earth, more specifically to gather evidence to confirm the theory of plate tectonics and document the history of the rise and fall of oceans and continents. I liked to think as well that our work would redound to the economic and environmental benefit of humankind. Our data could help unearth oceanic resources and safeguard national defense. That the U.S. Navy and the oil industry funded our work confirmed that basic research is not necessarily entirely altruistic. Where would the funds to run a ship such as this come from otherwise?[1]

---

[1] In 1970, the cost was $2,000 a day; in 2021, the coast of a day of ocean-going research ship time is at least $25,000/day.

Coming of Age Stories

My scientific colleagues were motivated by discovery. Our chief scientists had dedicated their lives to this difficult work. Nevertheless, increased undersea warfare capability and mineral discovery drove the funding that supports them. The funders received open access to the data. Our last chief scientist discovered two new oil deposits on the Argentine shelf that would benefit the Argentine economy. We were just cruising along analyzing subsea structure, and bang there were domes of salt rising through the subsea deposits. Salt dome topography can be associated with oil deposits. The discovery of the subsea salt deposits would enhance our chief scientist's reputation especially if the deposits turned out to be associated with petroleum resources.

Abidjan, Ivory Coast. The Ivory Coast was not what I expected. Gay barbers. A nightclub in a submerged submarine, the C105, which charged us (seven sailors and a French woman) $52 for drinks. Shoeshine boys dabbed polish at you as you ran away from them. One followed me a good mile outside of downtown to a park. I sat down with him and spread out a map of the Ivory Coast on the grass and gave him his first geography lesson. After that, he was my friend forever and whenever I approached the Hotel du Parc (Abidjan's Times Square, where the shoeshine boys congregated), for the rest of the weekend, he would come over, call me master, and keep the other shoeshine boys at arm's length.

The U.S. Embassy sat across the street from the Vietnamese Mekong Restaurant. My shoeshine friend told me that the American ambassador lunched there on Tuesdays and Fridays when he wasn't otherwise engaged.

Two bridges linked the modern French city of Abidjan with a vast adjacent African neighborhood, Treichville. Even in the modern city, people squatted on every patch of vacant ground, used eaves as shelter, or slept on their prayer rugs in the middle of the sidewalk. Abidjan, the Cannes of the Gold Coast; Treichville, the native market, the other people.

I stood on the bridge across the river watching the sun rise over this African city, when my shipmate Georges stumbled along, coming from the Abidjan side, shirt open, fly at half mast, piece of elephant tusk under one arm. He waved, "Hi!" then called, "Where's the ship?" He did not know that the ship had moved from the banana pier to the lumber pier.

We watch the sun rise from the middle of the bridge. Georges talked on and on about how drunk he'd been, how lost he felt when he thought he'd been left behind and he didn't know what day it was, and about how he'd paid $40 for his carved elephant tusk when he should have sent the money home to his wife and five kids.

Then he pointed to his wrist. "Look at that," he said. I looked.

"I traded my watch for a girl." Then he trotted off, muttering "Good watch, bad girl."

By this time, the sun had risen, and traffic had started on the bridge. Bicycles, motor bikes, foot traffic, women balanced towering loads delicately on their heads.

At seven a.m. I walked to the native market across the river in Treichville. It was mainly a food market: live chickens and turkeys abounded in rush cages; pig's feet were caked with mud and flies; there was an abundance of seafood. The stall keepers ate a mushy combination of millet and shrimps. The clothing stalls leaned heavily on bolts of cloth and cheap shoes. European products were sold and it was obvious from the number of stalls that the traditional colorful African cloth was on the decline. other articles for sale included housewares, such as heavy cast iron pots designed to be suspended over a fire, disinfectant, deworming medicine and so on. In a good hour of searching, I did not find even one item for sale that could be labelled "nonessential" other than a type of raisin bun.

The market had a cement floor and roof. It was hosed down every evening for sanitary purposes. But in the daytime the market was more crowded than a rush hour subway, with many people barefoot, and oblivious to the blood in the gutters and the pungent odor of foot-squashed chicken dung. It took a large dose of detached, objective determination to stand in the middle of this scene, the only white skin, and tell myself under my breath

Coming of Age Stories

that if I traveled across Africa I would purchase my own food from such scenes for a good many months. That sort of brief taste of the excursion encouraged me to plan carefully, cautiously, and exhaustively before embarking, and it made me very glad that I had the opportunity to ease myself into these conditions before I began my overland travels. The safety and relative comfort of our ship was only a few minutes' walk away.

Abidjan was certainly not the Africa I'd expected. Perhaps if I'd paid attention in college to my African geography text, I would have been better prepared because the city proper fit the chapter "urbanism in Africa" to a "T": an ultra-continental, fashionable, white elite, served and supported by local people who lived in far worse conditions.

We received mail in Abidjan, the first personal news in five weeks. Incredible things happen when twenty-nine people get notes from another world all at once. Everyone retreats to a corner of the navigation room (where mail is handed out). Shrieks and grunts and groans fly around like little missiles. All the little events of real life (as opposed to ship life) of twenty-nine guys for a month compressed into about thirty minutes in a noisy little room with a computer in it. One guy's wife had appendicitis and nearly died, another had a kid three weeks before, his first, a girl. He shouts and runs off the ship and doesn't tell anyone why or if he'll be back before we sail or what. He returns an hour and a half later with two Africans bearing a heavy crate, but he won't tell anyone what's inside. That night he breaks out the champagne and cigars and we all celebrate until the rosy dawn. Fine for the other life, but as for his present life, he won't see his wife or kid for at least three more months. He doesn't even know his new daughter's name.

We left Abidjan in the afternoon, crossing the estuary headed to sea. As the sun sank low in the humid air, the evening sky became gloriously lit. We bid Abidjan and its larger sister Treichville a fond adieu smoking cigars on the fantail under blood-red skies.

Charles A. Bookman | **The World Has Changed**

Science off the African Coast—Abidjan, Ivory Coast, to Moçamedes, Angola, Fall 1970.
We caught three sharks one night, an occasion for a blood fest. The sadists among us beat them over the head with fire axes. A lot of good it did. Their skin and skeleton were so tough our fire axes couldn't penetrate them. Even after repeated pummeling on the skull, they were still very much alive, writhing bodies somersaulting on deck with flashing jaws. One of our number dispatched a shark by driving a steel spike through the eye socket into the brain. We performed an autopsy in the interest of "science." Sharks are eating machines! Our shark specimen had gorged on juicy whole squid. I believe in catching fish and game to eat. I believe in catching one shark to see what's inside. Three sharks are a travesty serving no purpose other than showing us how dangerous it is to swim in these waters.

We ran seismic lines from the edge of the ocean basin up onto the shallow continental shelf off West Africa. We were interested in the depth of the sediments and in finding salt domes, which might indicate the presence of oil resources. We saw a great variety of wildlife on the continental shelf: three hammerhead sharks, a blue marlin, a sailfish, two sperm whales, some Portuguese Man o' War float by. (With the sharks and jellyfish, there was no swim station that day!) We encountered two manta rays, a sea cow (manatee), an Arab dhow, and a school of pilot whales! And albatrosses!

By Labor Day in the U.S., we were cruising just a few miles off Nigeria's Biafra province. It was the rainy season. Huge banks of cloud rested sullenly on the water surface. Just as the clouds dampened the earth, they depressed our spirits. When we finished the continental rise seismic lines, we explored whether a structural ridge ran southwest from the string of islands whose northwest outpost is Fernando Po. We would, in the next twenty-three days wriggle through the islands and southwest of them into deep water looking for signs of structural features beneath the deep sediments. One of our coring stations could show signs of high heat flow, so my data would be critical to mission success.

Coming of Age Stories

We celebrated Labor Day by working from dawn to dusk on three stations. Our present chief scientist ranked third on the list of 'core devils,' people who scheduled lots of deep-sea coring stations, just behind Dr. Maurice Ewing, the laboratory director, who sometimes stopped the ship five times a day for deep-sea coring, and Dr. Joe Worzel, who was avid about lowering the tripod cameras for seafloor photographs, which he sometimes called for as much as three times a day. Our chief scientist had good social skills, which helped a lot. Working sixteen hours a day is a breeze with a happy crew.

My boss, Dr. Marcus Langseth, had been encouraging me to apply to graduate school and to study heat flow at Lamont, which would have been very nice if that was what I wanted. Lamont led the country if not the world in geophysical research, but one of the reasons I took the job was to find out if scientific research would make a personally fulfilling career. I was pretty sure by this point in the oceanographic voyage that I was not cut out for theoretical research. One thing was positive, however. If I did change my mind and opt for theoretical science, geophysics would be a productive and rewarding field. I liked the travel and the intellectual inquiry, and I liked the full engagement that went with the field work.

By the time we reached Cape Town, South Africa, in November, I had worked at sea for eight months. There was no good time to leave a job, but the ship was going into dry dock there, and leaving in Cape Town—with a whole continent to explore— would be as good a time as any.

I had purchased excellent maps of Africa in Abidjan, Ivory Coast—detailed, explicit, and up to date. Michelin maps, certainly the best maps of Africa, had one shortcoming, the small scale. Even so, the three large map sheets included the most pertinent information—river crossings, petrol stations, and lodging.

At the time, I was mulling a six-month journey divided into two segments: Cape Town to Tanzania, and then, after some mountain climbing, Tanzania to Tangiers. Why break the journey in Tanzania? I was interested in climbing Mount Kilimanjaro and visiting Ngorongoro Crater and other game parks.[1] The most challenging stretch appeared to be from Khartoum, Sudan to Timbuctoo, Mali. At sea, I daydreamed over the maps. Detailed planning awaited at Cape Town, when I could realistically assess my resources and obtain better information about the many countries I might visit.

With the aid of the Michelin maps, I had an idea of the route: from Cape Town through the eastern edge of Lesotho. North through Victoria Falls, still north through the eastern edge of the Congo Basin, then turn east toward Nairobi, Kenya, crossing the rift valley with its lakes into Burundi and Rwanda. Take a break in the rift valley region. Hike in the Rwenzori Mountains in western Uganda, then climb Mount Kilimanjaro. Visit Ngorongoro Crater and other game parks and spend some time in the cities of Kampala, Uganda, and Nairobi, Kenya. Perhaps work in a game park for a season. I recall reading an article about the shortage of anti-poaching wardens because of the outdoor life they lead; this seemed at the time like meaningful work.

After Kenya, I'd head north towards Khartoum, Sudan then turn west towards Fort Lamy, Chad. Visit Lake Chad, then continue west to Upper Volta (today called Burkina Faso), then north to Timbuctoo, Mali and beyond, across the Sahara Desert into the Atlas Mountains, and finally to Tangiers, Morocco.

There were a couple of limitations to take into account. If I went solo, the cheapest way would be by motorcycle, but the cruising range was too small to cross the Sahara, and to spend much time in the Congo Basin. These vast areas, where gas stations were as much as four hundred miles apart, could be seen more effectively from a car, where you could carry spare parts and extra fuel.

Back to the present from my dreams of Africa travels, we were off the African coast in the rainy season. And when it rains in Africa, it just doesn't know when to stop. The sun hadn't shown

---

[1] More than fifty years later, in 2012, I climbed Mount Kilimanjaro and visited Ngorongoro Crater.

since before we entered Abidjan and it wasn't likely to return all month. Our next port, Moçamedes in Angola, was in a coastal desert so conditions were going to have to change somewhere along the way.

We crossed the equator and though we'd crossed it four times before, this time was for good so there was going to be a King Neptune ceremony. The sadists got ready. Mohawk haircuts, tar and feathers, everything as fraternity-like and unpleasant as you can think of. At the climax of the ceremony, a giant plastic barrel is filled with axle grease, sawdust, and kitchen waste, then a twenty-five pound brass weight is dropped into it. King Neptune's inductees are supposed to hop in and pull it out while blindfolded. Then pay homage to King Neptune—the fattest guy on board—by "kissing the brush." This, too, is really gross. They take a gigantic pipe cleaning brush, stiff bristle, coat it with axle grease then King Neptune places it between his legs and blindfolded you go up and kiss it and you're not supposed to know what you're kissing and get all kinds of horrible ideas, but everybody does, and it's all a hangover from the days when sailors put to sea for years at a time and all kinds of unnatural things must have gone on.

Moçamedes, Angola. Moçamedes[1] was quite a little town. Everyone had to receive a cholera shot before disembarking, so we all lined up at 8 a.m. to meet the Portuguese doctor. Thirty people onboard and the doctor brought ten needles, rusty and bent, about the size a cobbler might use. The captain asked the doctor if he had more modern equipment and if there might be another physician in town with more hypodermic needles. No sir. The first ten people went through the line and whined a little. Then the doctor dumped the needles into a paper cup and walked over to the coffee urn. He speared the paper cup with a

---

[1] In case you try to locate this remote port and railhead city on a map, Moçamedes was renamed Namibe in 1985; the name was changed back to Moçamedes in 2016.

fork and lowered it into the boiling coffee for ten seconds, then rinsed the cup in cold water. Thus, with the needles freshened (if not sterilized), he speared the next ten people. I was the twenty-ninth guy in line. We figured that by then we all had the same strains of hepatitis and other blood diseases, so diagnosis would be that much cheaper when we finally reached Cape Town.

At least that was the joke for half a day. Then people started walking back from town after two hours, their pierced arms bent at crude angles. "Can't move it," they'd say. And some started reporting fevers of 102 degrees. This disease business wasn't a rumor anymore.

Clueless about what was about to happen, I took my bicycle for a spin in the Namib desert outside of town right after my inoculation. Fifteen miles into open country, I saw ostriches and zebras. They were the only traffic in my three-hour pedal (the industrial traffic moved by rail). Arid, with mesas on the horizon, the Namib desert reminded me of the Dakota badlands.

I enjoyed my bike ride with the zebras immensely—until the fever and stiffness hit. I pedaled back to the ship one-handed. We learned later that the cholera vaccine is just tough to absorb. The inoculations put a big damper on our liberty. Everyone lay in bed groaning their two days away instead of celebrating ashore. The situation could have been worse as there wasn't that much celebrating to be done in Moçamedes, Angola.

Moçamedes was clean and charming. The dry coastal desert climate was pleasant. Rain was scarce, and the bay where the town was situated was beautiful. The town seemed more connected to the sea than the shore. Five blocks inland, the greenery and the sidewalks stopped and the Namib desert took over. Zebras ran wild, ostriches too.

Europeans occupied a very urbane core. I got a shave in the barber shop on the town square for 35 cents. The local people lived on the outskirts in mud and wattle huts or in caves dug into the sandstone cliffs that ringed the bay.

The town was a railhead for an interior mining district. Other industries included fishing, fish meal processing, and bird

Coming of Age Stories

guano. The locals did the manual labor. I watched a ship offloading corn. The sacks weighed two hundred pounds each. Two men to a sack, the human conveyor belt ran from dawn to dusk, fourteen hours with an hour-and-a-half off in the heat of the day. The workers earned about 60 cents a day. Elsewhere in the port, a crew was laying railroad ties. Twenty-seven workers lined up and at the supervisor's count they heaved a rail to their shoulders and ran in lock step to the laying site. They worked like this throughout the day, for similar wages.

Much of Africa dressed in repurposed western clothing, tee-shirts, old suits, and the like. The trading stalls in the markets were full of the stuff. We saw old First World War German army uniforms for sale as well as French and American surplus from the Second World War. Those double-breasted suits with heavy chalk stripes that every savvy American male disposed of about 1952, some of the workers in the port were wearing them. Did the designers for Brooks Brothers ever imagine that their double breasted creations would one day be worn by stevedores in a far-off Portuguese colony?

Angola, when I visited, was still a Portuguese colony though a guerrilla fight for liberation was in progress. Portugal's long-time dictator, Antonio Salazar had died just prior to our visit. Salazar once said, "I will only go to Angola when the last insurrectionist has been hung by the neck." Even so, townspeople still wore black armbands for their lost leader.

Moçamedes was a difficult liberty port because it was so isolated, and the colonialism and repression (and the lingering effects of the vaccinations) dampened our mood. We departed several hours early at the request of the police because several of the crew had wound up in jail, one for stealing a politician's gun, another because he was black consorting with whites (his fellow crew members).

I left Angola with a souvenir, a freshly killed zebra skin complete with ears and hooves. I wrapped it tightly in plastic. After we arrived in Cape Town, I consigned it to a taxidermist. Cleaned up, properly tanned, and sent home, the zebra provided years of costume fun. My wife and I would don it at Halloween and New Year's Eve parties. I would operate the front two legs, and she would bring up the striped rear.

As we left Moçamedes for Cape Town, South Africa, the captain advised us to avoid political discussions in South Africa. He hinted that anyone unfortunate enough to get thrown in jail for consorting with the other race might just be left there for a few days.

Five Weeks in the Roaring Forties. The sea was something to contend with. The swells were extraordinarily rough, swollen in passage up from the Antarctic ice. Our ship rolled from beam to beam, an angle of forty degrees. Temperatures hovered in the forties with wind and sea spray. The several hours a day that we worked outdoors were exhilarating, with gray, threatening skies, heavy rolling seas, and a brisk wind whipping the tops off the waves.

I figured there would be 400,000 40-degree rolls between Moçamedes and Cape Town. It wasn't a question of being seasick, rather, sick of the sea. You'd walk in your lab to find your instrument rolling on the floor in time with the waves. Apparently, it had been that way for five hours and no one had the courtesy to pick it up or at least tell me. We retreated into our own cocoons for self-preservation. To sit in a chair, you had to brace your feet at a wide angle on the floor as though you were a sumo wrestler. The cook's cake batter spread all over the oven. Someone else's bowl of soup might land in your lap. A gallon jug of Portuguese wine could jump into bed with you from the other side of the state room. My watch partner had a refrigerator fall on his head. Stepping outdoors became an exercise in frustration. The first wave soaked you from head to foot. Typing a letter took longer than usual as the typewriter slid from one side of the desk to the other. I pecked at the letters as they whizzed by.

This was albatross country. I counted fourteen soaring over our ship. There appeared to be three families: six adults, four juveniles, and four infants. Interesting that they stayed togeth-

Coming of Age Stories

er so. Floating on the water these birds looked like seagulls except for their monstrous size and long beak. When they took off, they were so large their wings blotted out the sun. Their wings were longer than a man is tall. They soared on the heat plume of the ship, dipping close to the waves then gliding through the vast troughs. When floating on the moving masses of water, they splashed around like mad ducks. I wondered where they nested. There were very few islands suitable for nesting, so they had to range thousands of miles.

This leg of the voyage crisscrossed the Walvis Ridge, which juts southwest from Africa toward the Mid-Atlantic Ridge. We were investigating the flow of very cold seawater (known as Antarctic bottom water) over the ridge. My instrument was crucial in the work as it gave a continuous temperature profile from the surface to the floor of the ocean. True to form, the Tgrad kept breaking down; I was kept busy keeping it running. In addition to my problems the ship had been a full year and a half at sea without being overhauled in dry dock. We were limping towards drydock in Cape Town with equipment failure of all kinds.

This was a hard-luck leg. Trying sea conditions made everyone ragged. It had been nearly two years since the ship and its scientific equipment received heavy, in-port maintenance. Everything, literally everything, showed wear and tear. The ship suffered a total power failure in heavy seas. We drifted and rocked and rolled for several hours. The seafloor cameras missed three stations. My seabed thermometer missed two and gave wretched data for most of the others. After I finally got it working right, the coring winch broke down.

Despite the conditions, there were interesting moments: For the first time in six months, our photographer captured a bottom photograph of a fish. It had eyes, even though there was absolutely no light three miles down. The fish was about 12 inches long, plus its long tail, and had large scales. We pulled up a forty-foot piece of seaweed with mussels on it. Laid out on deck, the mussels opened and closed their blue shells in unison searching for seawater. Their valves made a harmonious clicking sound.

Another type of flotsam was transparent and looked something like an ox tongue. It was flat, like the sole of a shoe, and wide. It had stubbly protrusions all over and it pulsated. When dried, the horns disappeared and gas bubbles formed. At night, the living forms were stirred up in our wake. They phosphoresced bright blue-white, like stars. We hauled in an itsy-bitsy hammer head shark. You could tell it was newborn because its skin, usually coarse and tough, was still soft and tender. Its teeth glistened like diamonds.

I completed my first oceanographic stint in Cape Town. Leaving the *R/V Conrad* in drydock, I embarked on a two-month overland adventure. I took a train from Cape Town to Johannesburg, hitchhiked around Natal and Pretoria provinces, and trekked in the Drakensberg Mountains on the border of Lesotho. Flying to Dar es Salaam, Tanzania, I visited Zanzibar, whose Maoist government had a loose confederation with Tanzania at the time. Returning to the mainland after exploring the island, I rode a train to the shore of Lake Tanganyika to visit the village where Henry Stanley met David Livingstone. I made my way from there to Lake Victoria intending to visit the Rwenzori Mountains, the famed mountains of the moon and source of the Nile. I ran out of money and time in Entebbe, Uganda. I would have to wait over forty years to visit the Rwenzori.[1]

East Pacific Rise, 1971

I returned to work as a seagoing electronics technician responsible for geothermal heat flow measurements at Lamont Geological Observatory of Columbia University (as it was known at the time) in the spring of 1971. I processed and analyzed the data from my six months on the *R/V Conrad* and prepared for another tour at sea. That opportunity came in November-De-

---

[1] The story of my 1970 Africa overland adventure is told in chapter 11. My 2012 climbing expedition to the Rwenzori and also Mt. Kilimanjaro will appear in the second volume of my memoirs.

cember, 1971 when I rejoined the *R/V Conrad* for the leg from Papeete, Tahiti, to Valparaiso, Chile.

A Fateful Airport Encounter. My flight to Papeete involved a short layover at Los Angeles International Airport due to a mechanical issue with the airplane. Pan American Airlines picked up the bar tab while we waited. I was traveling with Walter Pitman, our chief scientist. Walter was returning to a part of the ocean he knew well. While cruising across the East Pacific Rise on a previous voyage, he noticed that the magnetic data on the east and west sides of the ridge were mirror images. He took this as proof of tectonic spreading originating at mid-ocean ridges. The iron in the magma generated at the point of continental spreading aligned with the north pole as it existed at the time the magma cooled and hardened. Since the location of the poles has migrated and even flip/flopped over time, Walter was able to correlate the ages of rocks on either side of the ridge that cooled at the same time. He wrote his doctoral thesis on this novel confirmation of the theory of seafloor spreading. This was the start of a great teaching and research career. Walter was honored for his contributions to geophysics later in life with election to the National Academy of Sciences.

Over drinks, Walter described the "track," the route he'd mapped out for the *Conrad*. "What we have to do," he said, drawing on his napkin, "Is get from point A to point B, Tahiti to Valparaiso, pretty much a straight line across the East Pacific Rise. We're due to sail on the first, pull in on the thirtieth. And I don't give a damn what happens between now and then other than to gather good data."

"Isn't Easter Island between here and there?" I chimed in. Great tikis, no one that you or I know has ever been there. We could be the first, I thought.

"Sounds great," Walter said.

I forgot all about it, but I had planted a seed. Over cocktails with the captain one night in Tahiti, Walter mentioned that Easter Island was right on our track. The captain, always one for a lark, noted several obstacles: he didn't have a chart for Easter

Charles A. Bookman | The World Has Changed

Island, and the ship didn't have permission from the U.S. Navy for tourism, nor did it have clearance to visit the island from the Chilean government (these were the years of Salvador Allende's leftist government in Chile, and there was little love lost between Chile and the U.S. at the time). The captain solved one of the problems before we left Tahiti. He sent the third mate over to an island freighter to barter for an Easter Island chart.

Three Days in Tahiti. In Papeete, I could reliably find my shipmates at cocktail hour at Quinn's Bar of the Pacific. Quinn's sat right on the waterfront, with an unobstructed sunset view. I snapped one of the best photos of my life from my barstool. I have been to Tahiti several times since. Quinn's is long gone, and the famed view has become cluttered.

I planned a couple of adventures for the daytime. People think of Tahiti as a tropical isle and I suppose it is, but it is also, having risen from the sea, precipitously mountainous. I climbed Mount Aorai, one of its highest peaks, in the center of the island. The trail started out steep and became steeper. After a couple of hours, I found myself straddling a crumbling, slick clay ridge, making my way by shuffling my body along, gripping the ridge with my arms and my thighs. I resolved never to do that again!

Another expedition was more enjoyable. Four of us took a taxi to the northeast part of the island, where a dirt track rambled up the fast-flowing Papenoo River. We walked a couple of miles through banana and papaya gardens to the first waterfall, where we enjoyed a delicious cool swim. (Alas, you can't go home again. Nearly fifty years later, while visiting Tahiti in 2019, I drove up the Papenoo River only to find the riverbank a muddy desolate stretch of rock quarrying and other industrial activities. The waterfall was still there but I sure didn't want to swim in the river.)

On my final day, I circumnavigated the island on a moped. I found modest, friendly people and great scenery everywhere. I especially enjoyed the black sand beaches on the north side, near where Captain Cook observed Venus's transit across the face of the sun in 1769.

Coming of Age Stories

Crossing the Pacific from Tahiti to Chile. On our first full day at sea, we took one seabed core. A school of fish swam by while we were on station, a shark too—probably feeding on the smaller fish. No swim station that day! Mars appeared, a ruby red beam high in the night sky. Lamont seemed to be trying hard to improve conditions for its shipboard personnel. The rec room was equipped, music was piped into the galley, the first officer distributed a daily news bulletin, and there was a movie showing every evening. Little touches make a happy crew, and the amenities made it easier to get through the five-week voyage.

I noticed that our track would pass very near Pitcairn Island, where Fletcher Christian and the *HMS Bounty* mutineers burned their ship in 1790. Paul, a sailor, said the Austral Island group, 500 miles southwest of Tahiti was his personal paradise.

We scudded along in the trade winds. We celebrated the Chief Engineer's birthday, 58 years, a golfer and a sailor all his life. Louie the chief cook and Alex, our Goan assistant cook and steward set up a barbecue on the fantail. The wind blew our steak plates and cups around.

When we stopped to core the seabed at night, the afterdeck was floodlit. Squid and other marine life were attracted to the lights. Alex delighted in catching squid. He cooked them up in a mean curry sauce.

Latvian Independence Day (November 18) was another big occasion because we had several Latvians on board. My Latvian bunkmate and his two buddies downed what they thought was a fifth of vodka apiece. After they passed out, several of us helped them celebrate with the remaining third bottle, though we didn't tell them. When they sobered up, they found three empties, not two. They strutted around reminding all of us that "Latvians can hold their liquor." We didn't rain on their parade.

My watch partner was a Romanian refugee who most everybody else on board didn't like. He was about 40 years old, listened to Henry Mancini, didn't wear dirty clothes, or stand in drafts. Most of us were young and floating around; he was older and floating around.

Charles A. Bookman | The World Has Changed

I struggled to calibrate my Tgrad instrument. Without the calibration, the data was nearly useless. The machine worked on the seabed. All electrical connections seemed okay, but four successive calibration tests all failed. What could be wrong? Then it hit me, over a bowl of ice cream. The captain watched as I hollered and nearly dropped my bowl on his toe. "The water probe!" (The water probe measures ambient temperature in the surrounding seawater.) I'd forgotten to take it out of the circuit, so the ohms for the fixed resistor were wildly off. I felt like a lucky fool. The boss had spent 1,200 dollars to fly me out to get good data, then I brought up data that was practically useless because I couldn't make a lousy calibration film. What a relief. One of the things I liked about life afloat was the total involvement. I wasn't exactly a man possessed that last couple of days, but I did live, sleep, eat and breathe the problem, and the answer came over a bowl of ice cream.

The clock flew on November 4, 1971. I woke up in time to stand watch, then came station, then I worked right through until bedtime sixteen hours later. I constructed two thermal probes (the probes are strapped onto the outside of the core pipe). I repaired the electrical circuit that measured ambient pressure (a proxy for depth below sea level). We bent a pipe on station, "Tgrad bend," the core crew called it. They stopped speaking to me after that.

The core crew was quick and precise. Mike, from New Zealand, even hung over the side to tie the pipe down while you held his legs. He walked around in an old pair of gym shorts, ragged, ripped up both sides and the crotch so that his balls hung out to the wind. A real South Sea costume.

My poker game improved since my last stint at sea. I wore my red-flowered Tahitian pareu loincloth. The style spread; two other pareus appeared after I started wearing mine.

Over meals and in our spare time, we tossed around travel tales. The chief scientist rattled on about ports for hours, about guys blowing themselves up with half-pound charges of dynamite, about others who played football roulette with lit dynamite, about how one captain hornswoggled another out of two thousand pounds of prime beef for a case of rum. The patter was endless. Mike, the Kiwi core crew member had been in South Africa, Rhodesia and Mozambique. George the camera man had been to Ellesmere Island in the Arctic. Tales flew from all over.

Meals prompted their own form of travelogue. Our bread pudding was made with stale bread from three continents. Our thanksgiving turkeys were loaded months before in Australia.

"This Canadian maple syrup sure beats that artificial Japanese maple syrup we had on board."

"What Japanese syrup? I haven't seen any Japanese bottles laid out."

"Oh, it didn't come in bottles but in plastic bags. So, Louis [the cook] put it in the maple syrup jars from South Africa—look like peanut butter jars."

Horse radish from Australia, okra from Mauritius, mustard from Japan, fish from Japan, steak from Canada, grapes shipped air delivery from the U.S. No one onboard recalled where or when the Tabasco sauce with labels printed in French first appeared. Ketchup from Vancouver and Mexico. And condensed milk:

> Carnation milk is the best in the land
> Here I sit with a can in my hand
> No teats to pull, no hay to pitch
> Just punch a hole in the son of a bitch!

The star gazing was incredible in this untrammeled and untraveled part of the world. The Orion constellation was prominent on the stellar equator. I also identified Rigel, Sirius, Aldebaran, Betelgeuse the Three Kings, and the M42 Great Nebula, as well as a cluster of four spinning stars. Betelgeuse was the closest star to Earth and it's big. Sirius was the brightest in the whole sky. Despite all the successful sightings, I still found it difficult to pick out the Southern Cross in the night sky.

When the weather kicked up and the sea and wind tossed the ship about, there was more for us to do, like keep upright, look at the spumy panorama, save your equipment from bashing around.

Charles A. Bookman | The World Has Changed

Two weeks in, we were about as remote as you can get on this planet. We played a game of meridians—what we were aligned with, "Just passed Pasadena, headed for Needles." Also, Easter Island (Rapa Nui) shares longitude with Ogden, Utah, the Galapagos with Duluth, Minnesota. Working at sea was paradise for a geography major.

With the weather cooperating, we tacked a swim station onto our scientific station. I could see a hundred feet down. Lying on my back, I watched our small home roll gently, the only thing besides wavelet after wavelet on the limitless horizon. How perfect and perfectly calm it was to swim in this remote reach of the planet. Of course, one of the mates was watching with a rifle for sharks.

Eighteen days into our transit of the East Pacific, I felt the ship slow on the morning of Sunday, November 14, 1971. Dressing quickly, I noticed high clouds as I strode on deck. High clouds at sea are often a sign of land, and soon before us rose Easter Island. We anchored a half mile offshore of the small village of Hanga Roa and raised the semaphore that signals request for clearance. More than an hour passed—it was Sunday—before an open harbor launch headed our way. The captain and first officer bartered with the local health officer and Chilean customs officer. After the captain offered dozens of cartons of cigarettes, we were welcome to visit Easter Island for the day. Several open launches arrived soon after the deal was made, and we all went ashore, leaving only a skeleton crew onboard the ship.

The engine conked out in our skiff, so we rode the surf in. There must have been seventy-five islanders onshore to greet us and offer to help with our visit. The island residents hadn't yet become inured to tourists. They were open and instantly friendly. They wanted news, contact and conversation in addition to our dinero.[1]

---

[1] As for visiting Easter Island on an Office of Naval Research-funded oceanographic cruise, when Walter returned to work, Maurice "Doc" Ewing, director of Lamont and titan of geophysical oceanography,

Coming of Age Stories

The treeless hills behind Hanga Roa were ashen and bleak. Volcanic rubble was strewn all over, and there were occasional basalt outcrops. The volcanic soil produced good crops with water—but water was the big problem. Without surface streams, water had to come from wells. Where wells had been dug, bananas and pineapples grew, but the wells were few and far between. Mostly the landscape was dark tufts of wind-blown grass, pasture for horses and sheep.

There was no sign of industry. Fishing produced a meager livelihood for some. Over 2,000 miles from the coast of Chile, there was hardly any tourism. For the island residents, the cost of travel was an exceedingly difficult obstacle. There seemed to be little crime because there was so little to steal. The poverty we encountered was not the beaten down kind; it was more the absence of everything.

There were no paved roads on Easter Island in 1971, few tourists, and hardly any tourism. The government sponsored two plane flights a week. A government tourist hotel had opened just a month before our brief stop. There was so little on the island— no movie theatre and few stores other than to meet local needs. We traded clothes and cigarettes for trinkets. I traded a box of Tide laundry detergent for a stone ash tray. The locals' diet included fish from the sea, lamb grazed on the scrawny grass, and bananas and pineapples irrigated by the occasional well.

Those of us lucky enough to spend the day onshore had different ideas of how to see the island. Several people hustled off to drink homemade pineapple cognac. Some rode horseback. Two Land Rovers, affiliated with the new government hotel, were available to take people around to see the Moai statues. I toured the island on the fender of a tractor.

---

called him into his office to discuss the unscheduled stopover. "Do you know how much a day of ship time costs?" he lectured, emphasizing the negative image with the Navy and others created by this height of irresponsibility. Walter took his verbal licking then contritely got up to leave. As he reached the door, Doc said, "You know, Walter, if I'd been there, I would have stopped over too."

Charles A. Bookman | **The World Has Changed**

Statues scattered around the quarry

I had a dim memory that the most Moai statues were on the shoulder of a volcano crater at the far end of the island. A farmer drove three of us there on his blue Ford 3000 diesel tractor. We hung on to the fenders while the farmer took shortcuts so that we could see everything in a single afternoon. We zigzagged off-road and around ash mounds, over rocks and horse skeletons, past day-old foals, and young lambs nuzzling their mothers.

After an eternity of hanging on for dear life, we were surrounded by some of the most beautiful coastal scenery anywhere. Traveling along the slopes at the base of the volcano, we spied half-excavated statues. Oceanside, the breakers combed forty feet in perfect curls at the base of the coastal cliffs. Foam shot sky high as the waves struck. Rainbows formed in the droplets as the water rushed back out to sea.

What an incredible ride bouncing along the cliff edge on a tractor fender with horses running out of our way, surf breaking below, surrounded by statues from the past. Reaching the volcano, we lost count of the hundreds of statues littering the slopes. We climbed up to the lake in the volcano's crater. From the crater, half-finished and half-buried statues stretched as far as the eye could see. A rainbow arched overhead.

Following our day on Easter Island, we altered course to due east. The vessel really began to pitch and roll in the trade winds. I looked at the good-sized waves sending spray over our top decks. Most, almost but not quite, obscured the moonlit horizon. Lying flat on the topmost deck, I looked at the sky. Mars shone like a ruby off our stern.

When the sea kicked up, you always needed one hand to balance. Watch your step. Watch for falling objects and for stubbed toes. Feet don't seem to land where you intend them to. The sea was something else. Whitecaps, blown spray, foundering troughs between waves. You were on the fantail, say, looking out over the ship's wake. All of a sudden, you rode twenty feet up into the air. The ship sloped at a crazy angle behind you, going down, down, down. Next eye blink, you sank beneath the waves. Water rushed over the deck, the ship tilted at a crazy angle above you. What's this? I can't be riding that! Why, I'd be sick to my stomach! When the waves rock your world, objects roll off shelves, and equipment needs to be tied down. There was a wild spray panorama wherever I looked.

I tied my Tgrad down with elastic, then tried walking from one end of the ship to the other without using my hands. I failed. I even took an unplanned step or two on the walls. Toilet bowls slopped over every now and then. The cook's pots clattered around the galley. He was too drunk to notice, but nobody else had the key to get in and clean up.

Compounding the difficulty, we stopped to core the seabed eight times over the three roughest days. My machine failed twice, once requiring fourteen hours to make it run again. This was certainly no picnic.

After three days of tossing around, we broke into some good weather. "Sailing down a moonbeam" they call it when the moon breaks through the clouds and lights the way, dead ahead. The waves calmed some when the wind moved on, and finally we were left with a good blue sky, and giant easygoing Pacific swells, regular as the ocean itself.

Standing one six-hour watch each day in lieu of two four-hour watches means you have a little more free time to do things like spend four hours at the poker table. After winning twenty-five dollars one night—the big winner—I stepped out on the fantail to check the night stars. The moon wasn't up yet, but the sky was very clear. I missed our northern hemisphere constellations, Orion and the dippers especially, but finally found the Southern Cross. I took a leak off the fantail into the East Pacific. What a pleasure watching the phosphorescence leap up as you spritz the waves.

As our thirty-day transit of the East Pacific drew to a close we tried to squeeze in one final swim station before entering the cold Humboldt Current, which would make such pastimes much less enjoyable. The ladders were out, bathing suits were on, when one would-be swimmer spotted two sharks circling lazily about thirty feet away. That one was called off!

I left the *Conrad* in mid-December in Valparaiso, Chile. I was recalled for lack of supplies. Before returning to the US, I hitchhiked from Santiago, Chile to Buenos Aires, Argentina. That two-week adventure is recounted in chapter 11.

In the Mediterranean Sea on a French Oceanographic Vessel, April-June 1972

My next sea duty was a two-month scientific voyage from April to June 1972 in the Mediterranean Sea on the French oceanographic ship, *Jean Charcot*. We left from Tunis, Tunisia to gather seismic data in the western Mediterranean. We spent several days in Malaga, Spain and ended our voyage in Nice, France.

I arrived in Tunis several days early to get over jet lag before joining the ship. Never one to dally, I rented a car and drove southeast between the seacoast and the Sahara desert. I had neither map nor guidebook. Without either and unable to read the street signs, all in Arabic, it took me two hours to find my way out of town. I knew I was headed in the right direction when my road passed under the ruins of an ancient Roman aqueduct.

Mahomet, a tractor mechanic, was my first passenger. He was waiting for a bus, but I stopped for him. He took me to an

Coming of Age Stories

old bathhouse from the Emperor Hadrian's time (second century AD). The bathhouse was nestled beneath a cliff. We stopped at a nearby café for wine. Two others joined our table and discussed (in French of course) how best to spend my three days. My companions recommended the Roman ruins in Sfax and the beach at the island of Djerba. Two hours and two bottles of wine later, I continued down the road pausing for the night in the town of Sousse.

I stopped for another hitchhiker south of Sfax. Blond-headed Ezzadine was traveling home to attend to his sick daughter. He worked as a railroad engineer. His village lay five kilometers off the highway on a rude camel track. I drove him there. Most of the village turned out to be new government housing. Perhaps fifty tribe members idled outside the central souk. Ezzadine lived in a traditional compound outside of town. His wife cooked me a greasy egg in fig sauce. Out in the courtyard, his nephew chased a chicken and brought it to us. As Ezzadine prepared to slash its throat, my mind flashed to all the eggs that old bird would produce to feed Ezzadine's three girls and the momentary joy it might give him to feed me. I begged off the ceremonial meal and gave them the last of my homemade brownies. Taking my leave as gracefully as I could, I headed out through the date palms, figs, beans, grapes, sheep, goats, oxen, and camels, and back to the highway.

Outside Gabes, Tunisia, I passed cotton fields and vineyards. As I continued south, I began to see olives and almonds, even groves of date palms.

The ferry to Djerba comprised two dhows lashed together, powered by a one-cylinder long-shaft outboard engine. Two cars barely fit crosswise on the planks that were laid across the dhows. Djerba, Ulysses' legendary Isle of the Lotus Eaters had been reborn recently as a tourist destination for Europeans seeking sun and sand. An ancient fort with old guns guarded the modern souk with its hookah parlors and cheap tourist wares.

After a single night in a nearly empty tourist hotel, I returned to Tunis by way of Sfax. Sfax is dominated by a Roman colosseum that is in such good shape that it is still used for concerts and events. Returning to my car after visiting the colosseum, I became a little disoriented finding my way out of town. I ended up driving around a large central square several times looking for the road to Tunis. The sidewalks were crowded with people all of whom seemed to be waving at me with great anticipation. I learned later from the headlines that the president of Tunisia had just visited Sfax. The crowds were waiting for the presidential motorcade, and I was their brief amusement.

Aboard the Jean Charcot. I met the *Jean Charcot* and immediately plunged into an outpost of La Belle France. My fellow scientists spoke English like I speak French, which is to say haltingly. I communicated when I needed to find or do something. There was little idle chatter because of the language barrier, except at the dinner table where everyone tried harder. Looking for humor in my situation, I had thought they must speak some English or they never would have invited me. They must have been thinking, well, he must speak some French or he never would have come.

Life onboard was different from the Lamont ships. Here we were served by waiters and ate on white tablecloths. My cabin was paneled with dark wood. It was spacious, sported a porthole, and it was a double, though I bunked alone; and there was steward service, reading pillows and curtains.

The decks were wood. The dry lab was perched on an upper deck and featured a spacious layout and picture windows. Each discipline had its own lab, and the scientists didn't get their hands dirty because the sailors streamed the gear.

The *Jean Charcot* had so much superstructure that she wallowed in the merest swell. It was incredible how this wood-decked, white-hulled seemingly trim ship writhed about like a dying snake. When we weathered a full gale, two-thirds of the scientists took to their bunks.

We shot dynamite charges every thirty seconds to generate sound impulses for seismic study. The explosions hit the hull like a sledgehammer. I spent two hours a day suspended over the stern of the ship in a cage, like a crane control cab, dropping dynamite charges into a compressed air tube that ran behind the ship. If my timing was correct, the dynamite exploded at the end of the tube. If my timing was incorrect—well I didn't want to think about that. I handled more dynamite in a day than most terrorists see in a lifetime.

We ran seismic lines, spaced about thirty miles apart, from the middle of the Mediterranean up to the limit of navigation on the North African coast of Algeria and Morocco. We ran so close to land that the springtime green was vivid. We picked out wheat on the upland plateaus and vineyards on the steep slopes. Sometimes the mountains came right down to the sea. We identified the city of Algiers by its wispy plume of gray factory output.

Our scientific objective was to explore the ocean basins of the Tyrrhenian Sea. The bottom of the Mediterranean is underlain in many places with thick layers of salt—a relic of the ice ages when the sea was cut off from the Atlantic and evaporated to the point where today's seabed was a vast salt marsh. These episodes occurred several times in geologic time.

We encountered squalls every day and considerable waves. In the thick of one squall, a waterspout reared up on the horizon, fully formed, its spectacular blackness fulminating in conical anger, reaching between heaven and hell.

There was much marine traffic, mostly tankers and freighters. There was no sign of the great military fleets playing cat-and-mouse with each other.

Mealtimes were sacrosanct. On U.S. ships, you work all day and eat on the fly. They don't call the dining hall a "mess" for nothing! On the *Jean Charcot*, the work stopped at meal time. The meal, served by liveried waiters, usually consisted of five or six courses with wine, and ended with cheese and fruit, and a smoke on deck. The mid-day meal on May Day, a French holiday, was particularly memorable. The stewards wined and dined us through an eight-course meal. We started with pastis and pâté de foie gras to cleanse the palate, followed by an anchovy éclair and sole meuniere, each served with white wine. Then tournedos, salad, potatoes, served with a red Côtes du Rhone. After the obligatory selection of cheeses, we enjoyed omelette flambé for dessert, and finally cognac and coffee. Having properly celebrated May Day, the scientists gathered on the fantail for celebratory cigars. Then, and only then, did we return to work.

After three weeks of seismic work and excellent French meals, we called at Malaga, Spain, for recrewing and resupply. I walked all over town, ending the day at a wine bar complete with sawdust on the floor, peanuts, and happy people wearing berets singing for all they were worth. I enjoyed a few glasses of wine (at five cents a glass) with Helen and Beth, nurses from Montreal, traveling the world and working as nurses when they needed the money.

Back at sea off the western shores of Italy, I plotted my heat flow measurements on a map. I found patterns indicating higher heat conductivity over salt domes, and I engaged in several substantive discussions of my findings with French colleagues. It felt good to be able to communicate in a second language.

I mentioned that the scientists do science onboard, they don't handle the gear as scientists do on American research vessels. As a result, there are very few technicians onboard. Where talk among the scientific crew on American research ships is mainly whiskey and women, on the *Jean Charcot* it's whiskey, women, and science. This makes a great difference in attitude. The scientists are all eager to be here and interested in the day-to-day data, not just "doing time" for the money. Fully half the conversations that I was privy to were talking shop.

The French national laboratory Centre National pour L'exploration des Oceans (CNEXO) operated the *N/O Jean Charcot* as a cooperative vessel for all the oceanographic institutes of France.[1] Our six-week study of the Mediterranean was an annual

---

[1] CNEXO, the French national oceanographic laboratory, was merged into a new national oceanographic research institution, IFREMER, in 1984.

event. Most French oceanographers who conducted research in the Mediterranean participated. It was a yearly reunion of sorts. Together, they represented the Mediterranean research power of France. They collected the data together, did field analyses together, and talked shop for an entire month; this couldn't help but produce fruitful associations and greater research output.

Contrast this with Lamont where some researchers rarely went to sea, had little familiarity with field techniques and had the data gathered by people with little concept of the intended use or results. Lamont might have one scientist onboard at a time. Technicians are known for ingenuity and seat-of-the-pants thinking, but they might not have the depth of scientific experience or knowledge needed to capitalize on scientific opportunities that might arise at sea.

I departed the *Jean Charcot* from Nice. After visiting Marseille briefly with colleagues from the ship, I rode the overnight train to Paris, then continued on to London and finally Scotland in order to climb Ben Nevis, Scotland's highest peak. I hitchhiked from Glasgow to Fort William, the jumping off point for Ben Nevis, then from Fort William to Edinburgh. I climbed Ben Nevis in thick fog with a pick-up companion. We celebrated our climb in the pubs of Fort William, comparing blended and malt Scotch whiskeys. Returning to London, I flew to Bermuda where I reunited with my girlfriend Betsy Cheney. During our time at the Bermuda Biological Station, we planned a South American adventure, which is recounted in chapter 12.

Buenos Aires to Rio de Janeiro, Spring, 1973

Rough seas, twenty-foot waves, wind steady at 35 knots. These conditions held for days on end. Among our scientific objectives for this leg were mapping the many salt domes on the continental margin of the West Atlantic Ocean. Salt is plastic in the sense that it bends and moves under pressure, and the wedges, or domes of salt force their way up through the rock layers that underlie the seabed. Oil is known to pool at the upward thrusts adjacent to the salt. Many of the world's most productive oil fields, like those in the U.S.' Gulf of Mexico, are associated with salt domes. So our data would be of great interest to oil companies.

I was most impressed by the seabirds. We were accompanied by Argentine petrels, cape pigeons, and black mantled albatrosses. The sea water had to be nutrient-rich, with many forage fish for so many seabirds.

In addition to the birds, four sharks followed the ship. They sliced the water with their fins, just like in cartoons. They were accompanied by a school of dorado (sometimes called dolphin fish), the tastiest, meatiest little carnivore around. I hooked one on light tackle. I worked it gently. It cut the water from side to side, its silver scales flying. After some minutes, it weakened. Then my line snapped as I attempted to heave the bruiser aboard. Light tackle, big fish, the one that got away.

A Brief Visit Forty Years Later

My boss during my oceanology years was Dr. Marc Langseth, a geophysicist. Marc had grown up in the depression without a family. He took a great interest in his young technicians and graduate students, who he treated as his own made-up family. Marc was disappointed, I think, at my youthful coming and going and ultimate decision not to pursue a graduate degree in geophysics.

Marc invented the thermograd (the Tgrad), the instrument that measures sub-seabed thermal conductivity that I was hired and trained to maintain and use. His general theory, that higher heat flows would be found closer to the younger, thinner sediments found near seafloor spreading centers proved correct, but the heat flow data from the world's ocean basins never achieved the scientific prominence that other geophysical data did, such as seismic reflection and refraction, magnetics and gravity measurements. In addition to his work on plate tectonics, Marc and his team at Lamont designed the core drill used by the Apollo astronauts on the moon. He trained the astronauts in its use and in how to obtain good core samples. Marc achieved great renown from his lunar science.

Lamont acquired a new oceanographic ship several years after Marc's death in 1997. Designed for geophysical research, the ship was named the *R/V Langseth*. When I learned this, I wrote to Michael Purdy, the laboratory director, "Marc was my first boss and mentor. I'm curious about the renaming process. How did your fine new ship come to be named after Marc?"[1]

Mike replied, "We carried out a survey across the Observatory—got many tens of nominations for the name. Marc's was among them. For me, he exemplifies all that is great about Lamont. I first met him in 1974 and his widow Lillian remains a great friend of Lamont. I made the decision to move forward with the Langseth name, wrote up a rationale and got approval from the director of the National Science Foundation and the president of Columbia University. We will have a formal commissioning ceremony and will involve Lillian when the conversion process is complete."

When I learned in 2005 that the *Langseth* would be tied up for several months in Astoria, Oregon. I arranged for a private tour. To my surprise, my guide was an old shipmate, who was then Lamont's senior technician for seismic systems. The weather cooperated on the day I drove there (that is unusual for rainy Astoria). It was bright blue sky—in November. We had a great time swapping names and photos. I showed him a photo I had taken of him with long hair, playing guitar while transiting the Panama Canal in 1970.

---

[1] G. Michael Purdy's tenure as director of the federal National Science Foundation's Division of Ocean Sciences overlapped with my time at the National Research Council's Marine Board.

Chapter 11

Footloose in South and East Africa 1970

E wart Grogan took a gap year from Cambridge and walked the length of Africa from Cape Town to Cairo in 1900.[1] Grogan hunted from the Limpopo to the Nile. Fresh meat in the camp at all times! What sport, flushing the bok, the gazelle and the cheetah out of high grass.

Even then, the days of the great treks, of thousands of head bearers winding through tall grass, had passed. Two Cambridge chums were Grogan's only European companions. Of course he hired native guides and a small team of pack bearers and camp helpers. But there certainly was no serpentine throng of marchers.

Grogan encountered the local people everywhere, but his sensibilities were those of his imperialist age. Besides the stal-

---

[1] *From Cape to Cairo. The first traverse of Africa from south to north.* London, U.K.: Hurst and Blackett (1902).

wart Kalahari bushmen, Zulu corn grinders, Watusi herders, and strange Ubangi women, his photographs also show British colonials and her royal highness Queen Victoria's new telegraph installations.

I didn't exactly follow in Grogan's footsteps. South Africa, deeply racist at the time, was estranged from the rest of the continent. A backpacking, deeply tanned young American, I found it difficult to obtain visas in Cape Town, in part because of how I looked and in part because of the political situation between South Africa and the rest of the continent. Consular officials seemed suspicious of a young American traveling alone. This unanticipated hurdle shaped my journey.

Rock Climbing in Cape Town

My visa problems notwithstanding, I found Cape Town to be a wonderful city. Spreading over the flanks of nearby Table Mountain, between magnificent harbor and mountainside, the physical location was stunning. The view from Table Mountain took in the entire city and its surroundings. The climate was as good as it gets, though fresh water was scarce.

Cape Town was polyglot, with European, colored—East Indians, Malay and other East Asians—as well as Bantu (native) people). Despite the variety of people from many backgrounds, the government imposed strict racial separation. The Bantu overwhelmed all others in numbers. South Africa in 1970 had 16 million Bantu and 4 million Blankes. In the heart of the city you wondered where the Bantu were. They had been confined to isolated, segregated reserves on the outskirts of town. Drive there and you would see them. In contrast, country towns swarmed with Bantu. They gathered by the general store and the courthouse in colorful but ragtag clothes.

Bantus worked under permit for a year in Cape Town then returned to their homelands. Eight Bantus cleaned out our ship's fuel tanks. They worked in the foul diesel fumes of the empty tanks without respirators. Midst the metallic throbs of their work, we would occasionally hear guttural chants welling up from the pit. They used the walls of the tanks as drums. One worker led the wailing work song while the others scraped muck off the sides of the tanks. I noticed that the workers' supervisors took pride in speaking the native tongues. It seemed a rite of passage, interacting with your laborers on their terms.

Through the South African Mountaineering Club, I met welcoming climbers who showed me the ropes—literally—on Table Mountain. Joan Quail—fortyish, lithe and strong—was perhaps the best woman rock climber in the country. Lester Coelen, who was helping Safmarine (a South African shipping line) containerize their cargo operations, quickly became a boon companion. Lester was liberal racially, though he said he would never marry outside his race. Another climber, Mike Scott—very British, hip hip and cheerio—was an especially proficient rock climber. I found my "tribe" and others I met in Cape Town to be reserved but accepting of individual differences.

A companion from the ship met us one day on top of Table Mountain. We had climbed up, he had ridden the cable car. Unbenownst to my friends, my shipmate was high on mescaline. First thing he said to our group was, "I want to sleep in a cave."

"Jolly good show," Mike responded. "I know just the one. Gosh, I wish I could join you." He found my shipmate a cave to sleep in. No questions asked, nothing unusual at all.

The climbers called their girls dollies and birds. The women climbers were fit and good looking. The blondes tended to be of Dutch (Afrikaans) extraction, the black-haired red-cheeked women were of British heritage. In six hours of climbing on Table Mountain, I heard only two curse words.

The climbers were cynical about their country's racial situation. Equal jobs in South Africa did not equate to equal pay, nor to equal status. They talked about the profit to be made if you bought a "district 6" (a colored area just then opened to whites) house, fixed it up, and sold it.

Coming of Age Stories

Walking the Drakensberg on the Border between Lesotho and South Africa

Untangling myself from the ship, which remained in dry dock, I shouldered my backpack and headed off for several weeks of hitchhiking and plain old hiking adventures. The first leg involved a train ride to Kimberley of diamond pipe fame, then hitchhiking into KwaZulu-Natal Province, headed toward the Drakensberg mountains. The Drakensberg range forms an escarpment, a dramatic cliff measuring upwards of five thousand feet of elevation change. The escarpment runs for six hundred wild miles and forms the border between the land-locked independent nation of Lesotho (the uplands) and the province of KwaZulu-Natal, at the base of the cliff.

Being petroleum deficient, South Africa ran electric and steam engines on its railroads. I listened to the cinders from our coal-fired engine bounce off the roof as we steamed across the veldt. A gazelle (bok) ran with the train at dawn. Local people waved as we passed their isolated homesteads. Crossing the Orange River, I was reminded of the muddy Arkansas River as it flows through Kansas and Oklahoma.

What a railroad! My compartment was roomy, the bed comfortable. I enjoyed fine service in the dining car, where I met a student from the University of Cape Town. He was returning to Rhodesia, on summer vacation until March.

I noticed two types of native houses from the train, rondavels and squaredavels. Both are constructed with mud and wattle. They are roofed with thick thatch, not notched bundles as in Britain, but intricate lay patterns. There was also the occasional Zulu hut—woven reeds, like a giant overturned basket. Patterns in the straw.

I was supposed to rendezvous with my shipmate John Labrecque at Cathedral Peak Hotel in the Drakensberg mountains near the border of KwaZulu-Natal and the independent, land-locked nation of Lesotho. I arrived a couple of days earlier than planned, so made myself comfortable and set out to explore the mountainous surroundings. The park hotel offered cement rondavels with feather beds. There was a swimming pool and a trampoline. Guests were expected to dress for dinner. This was a tall order, given my backpacking wardrobe. For twenty cents extra, the staff brought the evening meal to my room.

After arriving and settling in, I walked three miles back down the road to the regional forester's office. I hoped he would have maps and local knowledge about hiking in the mountains, but I found he was more interested in cattle. "I never go to Cathedral Peak, mercy no, too much to do down here," he said. Most interesting at the station were the women in the nearby fields. Ten women worked the stony soil with wooden hoes. One sang out loud and bell-like, chanting to the sun, the soil, the warmth of the day. What a wail, rhythmic and pulsing. With every pulse, nine hoes flailed together at the ground, then rose in unison to await the next call. The women wore colorful, though ragged, clothes. Their bodies glistened, especially their shaved heads. The group effort lightened the hard work.

I hiked fifteen miles the next day across the fore-slope of the escarpment, climbing three thousand feet with a fifteen pound backpack. I climbed up one trail to a fire road, then followed the fire road left, over ridges and vales. I stopped at a rock outcrop to eat my lunch, fresh pineapple, purchased by the road the previous day. I twisted the pineapple open, then sliced the chunks off with my knife. After months of shipboard confinement, I was totally bushed and stiff by the end of the day.

My map showed another trail leading back to the park hotel via a different ridge. I followed the trail through two miles of high grass with fine views, then the trail petered out at an impressive 1,300-foot drop-off. The map showed a line of descent so I proceeded dubiously over precipitous terrain. I descended about 800' feet of bulging cliff face with my heart in my mouth. My route led to the top of an open notch in the cliff. I descended the next 500 feet using trees for handholds, with lots of air beneath me. I was stymied a few tens of feet from the bottom of the cliff. There seemed to be a possible exit involving a six-foot leap to a nearby tree, but I would definitely have only one chance. With rain clouds gathering overhead, I leaped—and lived to tell the tale.

According to my notes, I saw a four inch-long grasshopper, a family of ground hogs, a family of bok far off on open slopes, very graceful in the half light, and three snakes. Two of the snakes were poisonous but sluggish berg adders. The third snake was unknown to me. I almost stepped on it and it struck the heel of my boot.

Back at the hotel, another guest pointed out the correct trail to Cathedral Peak via Organ Pipe Pass and introduced me to John, the hotel's Zulu guide. I asked John about climbing Cathedral Peak. He told me he knew the hills, where to find Bushmen caves and cave paintings. As for the mountains at the top of the escarpment, "Not been that way," he said.

John the guide charged five rand a day, but I figured if he "hadn't been that way," I would do just as well on my own. I climbed through Organ Pipe Pass the next day, then turned right and followed the escarpment to its high point, Cathedral Peak (9,800 feet).

A short way up the trail I passed a Basuto farm tucked in between the ridges. A shepherd boy tending four cows nearby, pelted a berg adder with rocks. Ten minutes later I spotted another berg adder. Needless to say, I watched my steps from then on.

On the trail, I met Spud Williams, a Rhodesian, who taught biology at Michaelhouse School, a boarding prep school in Kwa-zulu-Natal. He was leading a group of schoolboys down. I also bumped into John the guide with a three-person party. Then I had the Drakensberg to myself. Climbing up through Organ Pipe Pass, I stayed left, which turned out not to be the best route. At a notch at 9,500 feet, my route became an airy knife-edge. From the summit, the sky extended forever over KwaZulu-Natal Province. The land dropped precipitously, losing 5,000 feet in elevation within a very few miles.

I encountered baboons twice on the way down. The first pack, a family of seven, sat on a pinnacle just off my descent ridge. I crouched behind a boulder and watched them for quite a while. I didn't immediately see the tough old alpha male baboon tiptoeing around me on the other side of the ridge. Was he going to roll stones on me or jump on top of me and then sink his impressive canines into my neck? Not wanting to find out, I lit out like a fiend for half a mile. The other baboon pack loped across a large flowery meadow, two on my left, three on my right. I walked right between them.

My shipmate John Labrecque showed up on my third day at the Cathedral Peak Hotel with adventures of his own to tell. He had gotten drunk with a gun-toting game hunter named Aubrey Smythe. Smythe had regaled him with wild tales of crocodile hunting and close escapes while on safari.

I had sussed out the route sufficiently so I felt ready to begin our backpack up into Lesotho, then along the escarpment crest to the next descent point several tens of miles along, by Tugela Falls, under Mount aux Sources.[1] We shouldered our heavy backpacks (mine weighed 60 pounds because it had all my belongings from the ship). We strolled leisurely up to a stream at 6,000 feet, then made camp with a wide open view of the next day's climb, retracing my steps 3,000 feet up through Organ Pipe Pass. We basked naked in the sun, swam in the stream, and watched bok up close and baboons from afar. I found a stone arrowhead in the stream. Given where I was, I realized it might not be that old.

Our five days hiking the Drakensberg crest are a blur of dramatic drop-offs on our right, rangeland on our left, and boulders and snakes along our route. On occasion, we encountered a working Basuto shepherd on horseback, wrapped in blankets to stave off the chill, or a stone kraal and rondavel, occupied seasonally when the herds are in the high pastures. My field notes include the following anecdotes and impressions:

---

[1] Tugela Falls in Royal Natal National Park would be the world's tallest waterfall if it ran consistently all year long.

Coming of Age Stories

–Evening of first campsite, three Basuto women, three men walk by in city clothes, suitcases in hand, as though going to the train station. I would not have believed they'd walked like that 140 miles from the interior of Lesotho to work for the season at the Cathedral Peak Hotel unless they had told me. The women approached first; the men thought we might be border police. We called to the women, they responded from the other side of the stream, "How are you momsa [memsahib, sir]?" we offered tea, but they continued on their way. The men came next. They stopped and shared our tea. Two of them had worked at the hotel before. The third was younger, almost a boy. He was wrapped in a blanket. From the way he stared as he looked around our campsite, he was clearly a first-timer.

The Cleft Peak Drakensberg

–First day's hike, long pull up through Organ Pipe Pass and then onto the ridge crest atop the Drakensberg escarpment. High meadows bursting with spring flowers, baboons nearby. Took hero photos on the summit of Cleft Peak. John and I became separated earlier in the day, found each other by sheer luck just as the fog rolled in. While alone, I nearly stepped on a snake. The snake was grey with wide yellow stripes on each side. Was it a cobra, berg adder, or puff adder? I was in a steep couloir on the face of the escarpment and wouldn't have been found. Fog for lunch. Route finding begins to be fun. Keep the escarpment on your right!

Charles A. Bookman | The World Has Changed

Use the compass and contour, balance minimum work with maximum views. Herds of horses up here and of course their herders. Stone kraals. Slopes studded with flowers purple, red, white, yellow, like miniature carnations—dandelions, buttercups, African edelweiss.

–Pick up the "Lesotho National Road", a horse track, after two hours of walking on our third day. A series of barely discernible mildly eroded ruts crossing the flowered slopes. Erosion everywhere. The alpine topsoil is very delicate and is being overgrazed. Encounter shepherds on the road driving mules with large sacks of grain. They are headed to their stone huts and kraals for the summer grazing season. The national road actually goes somewhere beyond the pastures, the village of Witsieshoek several days away.

–That afternoon, some native women offered us Tswala (kaffir beer). Looks like chocolate milk. Sour but refreshing. Took their photo (snap!) with their men. Women are well dressed and clean. Men wear pants with a blanket draped over the shoulders. Shoes are incredibly old. Many wear rubber boots. Poor men walk beside their mules. Better-off men ride a mule. The wealthiest men ride horses with saddles. Every native we met wanted a cigarette.

The Chain Ladder Drakensberg

Coming of Age Stories

–Final day on the ridge crest and we're wreathed in thick fog. Stumble onto a native hut inhabited by Muhau and his talkative, capable wife. For 50 cents, Muhau guides us at a furious pace to Mont Aux Sources hut and the chain ladder that descends the escarpment. We take photos. We offer him dates. From his quixotic reaction, they might be his first sweets. Muhau's footing is really good; he knows his meadow. Descending the chain for hundreds of feet with backpacks midst swirling fog—an experience not to be repeated! At the bottom, there is a new road and trash cans, the first signs of civilization after days in the high meadows. We follow the road under a hot sun. Our feet are tender after days of punishment. I have renamed my Austrian Penzl boots "Painsall." At 4:30, we turn onto a trail to Tendele camp in the national park. Our morale is low. We stumble on a tree-filled gorge with a stream at the bottom. Higher up above the stream, there is a huge rock cave. We make camp in the cave.

–5:30 AM a bok walks right by our cave, maybe 10' away. We walk out later to Tendele, where we make friends with the chief ranger who's walked the escarpment all the way to Sani Pass and has drawn an excellent map.

After walking out, we spent the evening in a pub in Estcourt. We drank with the local Afrikaners, who played killer darts. We met Guis the carpentry teacher; Lou the town greaser; Charlie who got stuck with a bayonet at 'Mein (El Alamein) so he missed the 'Brook (Tobruk); and Tomi the lady killer. Also Tiny the Hindu barkeep, who was more of a lush than the guys he served. Fights broke out, just like at home.

Parting from John for a few days, I hitched a ride out of Estcourt in the back of a Hofinger, a miniature all-terrain pickup. My ride, a young couple from Vreiheid were obviously in love with each other, their country, and the earth. They shared their knowledge of the local plants, wildlife, and history. We stopped at monuments from the Boer War and even visited the place where the Boers captured young Winston Churchill off an armored train. We had a lovely time and I thanked them profusely for the sightseeing and the pleasure of their company. They apologized for making so little forward progress.

The South Africans I met seemed lonely. The bars were full of single men and unhappy couples. Salesmen talked compulsively (I guess they talk compulsively everywhere). Lots of conversations involved expressions of fear or hatred. The Boers, the English, the coloreds, they all were wary of the other.

Kruger National Park

I reunited with John Labrecque in Johannesburg, South Africa in order to tour Kruger National Park by car. After days of hitchhiking, what a pleasure it was not to have to discuss the performance of obscure brands of gasoline in even more obscure cars, or to hear about the jockey shorts business in Bloemfontein. Or to hear how drought has hurt Briggs and Stratton sales in Kimberley. Or how Edgar's Department Store of KwaZulu-Natal must move their entire inventory by December 18 or file for bankruptcy. Not that I wasn't interested, mind you, but there are other things in the world: the land, the people. Truly interesting and engaging rides, such as with the young couple who had picked me up in Estcourt, were few and far between.

Our first night in the game park, we heard hyenas and lions from our rondavel. Touring during the day, we saw vervet monkeys, chacma baboons, dwarf mongoose, elephants, Burchell's zebra, hippopotamuses, warthogs, giraffes, steenbok, duiker, Sharpe's grysbok, oribi, roebuck (not Sears), waterbuck, impala, sable antelope, black wildebeest, bushbuck, nyala, kudu, African buffalo, and even the vaunted bush squirrel.

We had two odd wildlife encounters. In the first, we startled an elephant standing in the shade by the road. Reluctant to approach too close, I used the clutch to crawl toward her. Wrapping her trunk around a nearby tree, the elephant sent a warning shot in the form of the tree trunk across our hood. I quickly shifted into reverse. Later that day, in the heat of the afternoon, we drove by a stretch of roadside in flames. A lone giraffe watched the fire from the shade of an acacia tree a short distance away. Using our boot heels like shovels, we kicked a fire line between the flames and the giraffe. This was hot sweaty work. Eventually a ranger came along. He told us we had just interfered with a controlled burn and fined us fifty rand.

The difference between a game park and a zoo is quantity not quality. You see more animals, and their poses are more natural, but really it is only day sightseeing. As remarkable as the game park is, I did not feel as though I was "on safari" in Kruger park. It is much more exciting, for me, to walk in nature than to view it from a vehicle. The real wild. Baboons stalking you, sharing a meadow. Such encounters are different from the game park experience.

As for other wildlife, several KLM stewardesses were staying at our camp in the park (Pretorius Kop). They didn't speak much English. We lay in the sun with them and shared good South African wine, which we had picked up for thirty-seven cents a bottle. After three bottles, we thought pronouncing "Hippopotamus" in Dutch was the funniest thing in the world.

I tried to trade my Japanese cook's knife to our cook boy for his arm bracelet. He really wanted the knife, but was unwilling to give up his bracelet. Turns out the bracelet was his tribal puberty bracelet and identified all his circumcision brothers.

Headed to Botswana but Stuck on the Side of the Road

After the game park, I struck off hitchhiking again, this time west toward Botswana. Not too long into my journey, I got stuck by the side of the road. This was the first time in three weeks of hitchhiking in South Africa, but wow! when I get stuck, I really get stuck. I spent the night in a motel a hundred yards from the Orange River. I considered camping on the banks with two vervet monkeys, but the bugs looked a mite large.

When I finally caught a ride the next morning, the driver taught me the Lord's Prayer in Afrikaans (Psalm van David):

Die here is my herder; niks sal my ontbreek nie
Hy lagt me neele in groen weivelde; nae waters war rus is leihy my heen
Hy verkuik my siel; hy lei myin die spare van geregtigheid, om sy naam ontwil.
Algsam e kook in 'n dal vandoodskaduwee, ek sal geenonheil vrees nie; want u is me my: u stoke n u staf die vertroos ny.
U berei die tafel vor my aangesig teenoor my teestanders; u maak my hoof vet met olie; my beker loopoor.
Net goldheid en huns sal myvolg al die dae van my lewe; en ek sal in die huis van die here bly in lengte van dae.

I tarried in Mafeking, known for its "big hole" diamond pipe. The miners come from the native reserves. After signing up for seven-month stints, they are assigned to "hostels." They do not have the freedom of the town.

I hitched on the corner where the mine workers, released from their service, find rides back home. No one stopped. Eventually, I realized that the African drivers would not pick up the mine workers with me there, and the white drivers would not pick me up with the Africans there. So, I picked up my pack and started to walk out of town into the Karoo Desert. This turned into a two-day dry spell without rides and a long walk across the unremitting desert. South of Hopetown was fiendish: the heat caused me to see double by 8 a.m. The Karoo looked covered with slick wet red clay, but it was a mirage. I counted nine large termite mounds in my field of view, I knelt to touch the soil, a fine powdery almost talc-like red dust.

I never made it to Botswana. I turned around—literally—at the border. I caught a ride finally with Roger, an American. He drove me all the way to Cape Town and another world. I told him he might have saved my life.

My favorite areas in South Africa were KwaZulu-Natal and southern Cape Province. I had experiences running the gamut from a .45 pointed in my face by a big game hunter to eating home-baked holiday goodies in an Afrikaans home in Mafeking, and even the tourist experiences like Kruger Park. As for the apartheid that prevailed at the time, I sensed every day the fear in the white people I interacted with, and the general instability in the society. The challenge for the country would be to chart a realistic path forward. Incredibly, wise leaders were able to do that.

Zanzibar Story

Tanzania was the first African country I could enter from South Africa without a visa. I purchased an air ticket to Dar es Salaam. The culture shock was immediate. In South Africa, I couldn't dine with people of another race. In Dar es Salaam, I shared a hotel room with two Africans. One of my roommates was studying to be a medical lab technician. It was hot and humid. The thermometer read eighty degrees at 11 p.m. We slept under dome-like mosquito nets without a breath of air stirring anywhere.

I flew the short hop over to Zanzibar in a German-operated Fokker F27, a sturdy workhorse aircraft with wings mounted high on the fuselage. Zanzibar in 1970 was in a loose political affiliation with the former Tanganyika on the mainland. Its government was Marxist, while the rest of Tanzania under Julius Nyerere was more socialist and tolerant.

Stone Town's narrow streets intersected and interconnected like a snarled tangle of newborn snakes. From Beit-al-Ajaib, the house of wonders, I walked left and in to the nest. Ali Baba hold back. Lucky Charlie is ready to take on what you can give. The narrow streets were busy. Model T's (even saw one driven by an aged Hindu with a red "L" plate in the rear) roared down the alleyways. Be quick. Jump into doorways or open sewers.

Watch the doors. Stone Town is famous for its ornately carved wooden portals, many with sharp knobby protrusions. Some are adorned with old, rusty spikes. Don't get too close. There are all sorts of sights. Palaces by the sea, built by sultans, many from Oman. Some have deep, capacious basements, legacies of slaving.

Zanzibar was the third largest producer of cloves (after Indonesia and Madagascar). At harvest time, the streets and roadsides were strewn with drying cloves and the air was filled with their aroma.

They drove fiendishly. The rule seemed to be never hit the brake sooner than the horn. The exception was one-lane bridges; make sure you are at least halfway across before you brake so the other guy has to back up. The buses when I visited were lorries filled with people and even donkeys. Large bunches of bananas were strapped to the roof.

I took a 25-mile walk counterclockwise around the island, completing a loop that touched the beach at Bububu. I used my limited Swahili to greet passersby. "Jambo" means "Hello." "Jambo abari" means "Hello, how are you?" "Salaama" is a universal greeting; it means "health." "Karibe" means "you are welcome," or "at your service."

Two students on a single bicycle were curious about me. The first student spoke good English. He invited me off the road to see his house. "This is a clove tree, these are limes. Between banana trees we plant casavas." His house, like all other houses in the neighborhood, was made of stick frame with woven palm fronds on the outside. I took a photo of his grandpa squatting on the ground (how many western grandparents can squat like that?).

Several miles further, past grove after grove of tropical forest crops, I fell into conversation with Usuf, a researcher at the Agricultural Experiment Station. Usuf spoke English well. He had studied agronomy at Punjab University in Lahore, Pakistan. He managed fifteen acres and complained that the present Marxist government didn't support research. He pointed out abandoned groves of cloves and bamboo planted by the British that lay waste. He identified many tropical crops: cassava, ground nuts, sisal, ylang ylang, coffee (robusta), cloves, rice, coconuts, obscure citrus, pineapples, and cacao. His helpers were cutting open cacao pods just as we arrived. The seeds inside the pods looked like a cross between oysters and Brazil nuts. They tasted like unsweetened chocolate. Before drying, the seeds are cut from the pod and then fermented.

We walked by a prison camp. No wire, no guards. Fine new housing. The prisoners' families live with the prisoners. As Usuf put it, "Zanzibar is an island. No one can escape anyway."

Usuf asked me what a hippie was. I said, "A hippie is an American who would be happy living in Zanzibar where he could pick each meal off his trees." He seemed satisfied with my answer.

I met Mohammed, another student, an hour later in Mbusimi. He took me off the road to his house to meet his father and six or seven attractive siblings, most of them beautiful Arab girls with glossy dark hair and mellow skin tone. I was asked not to photograph the girls. Mohammed offered me lunch. The smallest boy shinnied up a palm tree and lopped off three coconuts while the girls ran off to gather exotic fruits. Mohammed proved expert at opening the coconuts. The nuts were very different from those you buy in a store. They were sweet and full of milk. The meat was soft, ripe and gelatinous, not old, dry and cracked. After the meal I watched Mohammed pray to Mecca. I gave sideways glances to his attractive sisters and they glanced demurely back.

Bububu Beach had been turned into a resort when I revisited Zanzibar in 2012. When I visited it with Mohammed in 1970, it was pristine, home only to a few fishing dhows. The sand was white, the water warm and aqua-colored. Sea and sky stretched above and below us forever as we swam with complete abandon.

It seemed that Zanzibar's Marxist leaders believed that as long as there were no rich people, there would be no poverty, or at least the widespread poverty that there was, would be less noticeable. The soil was productive. Everyone could eat their fill from the forest or the sea, and they picked a little more for the cash economy. Maybe that was why the government was for isolation and against Usuf's research and change.

Education was ubiquitous. I was surprised at how much English was spoken. The only truly impoverished people I saw were those in town who had left the land and not found other work.

The "Peoples' Revolution" of 1964 that ushered the Marxists into power brought changes in land tenancy. Before the revolution, there were many absentee landlords. Following the revolution, every farmer worked at least three acres. While their crops were bought and sold freely on the island at the time, exports were handled through state corporations.

My time in paradise was cut short by the Tanzanian government. One of my walking companions informed on me and I was visited at my guest house by a functionary who told me that I no longer had freedom of movement. I had two days to depart Zanzibar. My movements in town were tracked by someone from internal security until I did in fact depart.

By Train Across Tanzania

Back in Dar es Salaam I shared a hotel room with a Swede who raised sisal near Morogoro, Tanzania. After he told me stories of how he shot the toes off Africans he found setting fire to his sisal plants, he asked if I would like to work for a week or two on the plantation as an overseer; shooting toes, I supposed. Not knowing my way around a firearm, I declined his offer of temporary employment.

I enjoyed the inexpensive, plentiful Indian restaurants. For five bob, I sat down to a vegetarian meal served on a tray the size of a large pizza that was a veritable orgy of spices and tastes. Bean soup, two types of curries, Vhaji (a cabbage dish), small pickles, onion peppers, ginger root, yoghurt, roti (sort of southern fried matzoh), rice. Food like this is savored twice; first on the way in, later on the way out.

I traveled by train two days across Tanzania to Kigoma on the shore of Lake Tanganyika. Kigoma is near the fishing village of Ujiji, where the explorer-journalist Henry Stanley met the impoverished and ill missionary, David Livingstone.

At Kigoma, I pondered my choices for the rest of my time in Africa. I could ferry across the lake to the republic of the Congo. From there, I could visit the Virunga Volcanos—home of the mountain gorilla—and then ride a boat down the Congo River. That would be an odyssey to remember. Another ferry ran north up the lake towards Burundi. That would be another approach into the Central African mountains. A third option would be to backtrack on the railroad a bit, then cut north, crossing Lake Victoria by ferry. From there, I could proceed west into the Rwenzori Mountains, the fabled Mountains of the Moon and source of the Nile, which straddle the border of Uganda and the Congo. After the Rwenzori, I could follow the Nile River north through Kenya, Sudan and Egypt.

Counting my remaining funds and reevaluating my isolated situation. I wrote my parents from Kigoma: "I don't enjoy train riding and hitchhiking for the sake of train riding and hitchhiking. I do them because they connect me with the people. This worked in South Africa largely because of the minimal language barrier. The situation is entirely different in Central Africa. I do a lot of smiling while those I smile at stare at my impressive footwear (hiking boots). Most of what I learn comes through seeing, not through conversation. Since the language barrier will be even greater in the Congo or Burundi where French (not English) is the second—or third (behind Swahili) language, I have decided to head by train and ferry to Uganda. More generally, I plan to truncate my journey. After seeking out the mountains, I will fly to Khartoum, then ferry down the Nile. Traveling overland with a 60 pound backpack is hard work and can be dangerous at times. The risks are physical, bacterial, and human. The reward is experiencing the world in the richest possible way."

In the end, running out of cash and feeling quite alone, I truncated my journey. I visited Uganda briefly and then flew home.

"Mr. Livingston, I Presume"

The railroad across Tanzania ends at the port of Kigoma on Lake Tanganyika. Ferries on the lake, when they run, connect to the Congo (West), Burundi (North), and Zambia (South). I spent several days at a guest house in Kigoma mulling my options. The guest house served the same meal every evening, native rice and curried goat. I suppose this was because travelers are supposed to travel, not stay for days on end as I was doing. The lake glimmered 200 yards away, at the end of the street. It stretched long and narrow north to south, not much wider than Long Island Sound. I could make out the Congo on the far shore. The houses in town were primarily mud and sticks, with palm thatch or tin for roofing. It rained a lot.

I walked to Ujiji one morning, the village where, in 1871, Henry Stanley met David Livingstone "under the mango tree." Livingstone was sick with malaria and had been pronounced "lost" in the western press. The meeting place was just above the muddy port. Local fishermen cleaned and repaired their nets at the spot. There was much noise and local color as fish was sold there as well. When I visited, an inscribed obelisk marked the spot.

Hanging around the fishing port, I played hide and seek with a five-year-old. His parents were greatly amused.

I had walked for an hour or more along the road to Ujiji. I resolved to make my return along the undeveloped lake shoreline. I followed the shore to the point of the peninsula that separates Kigoma and Ujiji.

Most of the shore is high bank, about fifty feet high, of red pebbly stone, with grass on top. There are occasional pebble beaches. The largest of these lay by a fishing village—rather large and extraordinarily primitive, though the mud huts showed some signs of an improving economic position. Some huts had a new door, others a glass window. Ground cassava dried on straw mats in front of every hut. The villagers bathed on the pebble beach. I watched two native girls play in the water. They didn't care in the least that I passed by. In fact, they might have considered it odd that I didn't join them.

Further along, I came to a dirt gully bisecting the cliff. It offered steep access to the pebble beach below, I descended the gully at my wary pace. (A combination of small steps and large eyes, a friend once said of my wary pace, "Caution and safety run second nature in your movements.") Some thirty feet into the narrow pebbly gully, hanging onto a leafy tree for balance, feet resting on a thick, sturdy flowering plant, a largish lizard darted into the lush foliage, moving from the center of the gully. Though obviously no threat, the lizard's non-blinking eyes honed my perceptions of gully life. I now knew what to look for. Two steps further down, my caution was amply rewarded. Never before in clear daylight have I seen such a sight. It was as thick as my upper arm, and its color scheme ranged from dark green on top to yellowish on the under belly. I cannot begin to guess its length because its head disappeared into the foliage on one side of the gully while its tail knotted into the underbrush on the other. It perceived me at about the same moment that I perceived it. Immediately, both sides of the ravine were alive with rippling movement. Not only was it long enough to stretch across the gully, but its body ran into the trees and bushes on either side. Although I could not see it, its fanged head could well have been right beneath my elbow or within inches of the still-staring lizard.

I bounded up, back the way I had come, on to the short grass at the top of the gully in no more than six steps and fewer seconds. It may have been a green mamba. These snakes grow to seven feet and enjoy draping over things as this one was. As for its venom, a fierce, front-fang-delivered nerve toxin unlike any other in its speed and total effectiveness, it is said that once bitten you may have enough time to get down on your knees and start reciting the Lord's Prayer, but along about "Thy will be done," the convulsions begin. The mamba may not even have released its fangs yet.

I returned somewhat humbled to Kigoma, my mind made up, looking forward to my evening repast of rice and curried goat, and eventually a train ride to the shore of Lake Victoria.

My Africa overland adventure notes end at Kigoma. I took trains and a ferry to Entebbe, Uganda and then returned home to New York City. It was a good thing that I wrapped up my travels in December, 1970 as Idi Amin seized power in Uganda in a coup in January, 1971 and the country descended into years of bloody chaos. If I had continued on to the Rwenzori Mountains, as I had dreamed, I would almost definitely have been in Uganda when the coup took place. I consider that a bullet dodged.[1]

---

[1] More than forty years later, I was lucky enough to return to Entebbe, Uganda and travel from there into the Rwenzori Mountains. With my son Zac, we completed the fabled central circuit, a week-long trek through rare alpine bogs and over glacial peaks. That story will be told in the second volume of my memoirs.

Chapter 12

Hitchhiking Across South America 1971

Valparaiso, Chile careened down coastal bluffs. When the *Conrad* called there in December, 1971, cable cars and elevators connected the busy waterfront downtown to the residential neighborhoods perched precariously on the bluffs. Depression-era automobiles, European cars from the 1930s, plied the streets. Chile's leftist, democratically elected leader Salvador Allende had just hosted Fidel Castro. The people were still celebrating. Banners across the main street proclaimed the solidarity of the Chilean and Cuban people.

Inflation was out of control. If you paid with hard currency beers were three cents and bottles of good Chilean wine were twenty cents. Sailors on liberty, we made good use of our providential purchasing power. Between the hills, the long awaited shore time, and the celebratory mood of the Chileans, there was a cockamamie energy in the air. Anything could happen.

Charles A. Bookman | **The World Has Changed**

Valparaiso was a port city with lots of lonely boys coming in on big ships. While waiting at anchor for clearance to dock at a pier, a motor boat putted up alongside with seven women dancing on deck to a radio. They waved and shouted "Hi, Yanquis." Shedding their blouses, they swung alongside just long enough to drop off their calling cards; *Louisiana Hotel—Girls to serve you anytime.*

Our first night ashore, Charlie Brown, a South African engineer, bought out the bar at Yocko's. (Charlie Brown spoke three languages, none fluently. One night at sea, the chief engineer asked Charlie, "Are you cussin' me out in Dutch?"

"No, Swahili," he said.

Buying out the bar at three cents a beer and five cents a glass for wine, you can't go wrong. At those prices, buying out the bar for an entire evening hardly cost a week's pay. By the time we arrived, Charlie had spent maybe fifty cents on himself and he was having trouble standing up.

Yocko's was that kind of place. An interior balcony ringed the upper walls. In addition to providing access to bedrooms for the working girls, you could look down on the action from there. The second engineer made off to a balcony bedroom with a girlfriend. Not long after, our captain, a dead ringer for Commander Schweppes, strolled in with a very attractive, mature woman on his arm.

The second engineer stepped out on the balcony without his pants while his gal was jumping down the stairs. "Stop thief," he howled, "She took my money." The woman made it to the bar waving a hundred dollar bill. The second engineer stayed with her all weekend trying to get his money back, or at least a full return on his investment.

I mostly watched the show—at least until crazy Maria (jet black hair, medium build, slinky black dress) came over to me. "Come to my place," she said, "Across the street. I have marijuana, rock and roll. You feel at home."

Maria had a nice little place. We hung out the second-floor kitchen window watching the street life. She had her whole family back there. Her kid, four or five years old, dunked bread in soup. She kept her marijuana in the kitchen jar labelled "Flour."

Maria opened the ice box: it was an actual ice box, not a Frigidaire. She served lemonade, and looked at me in silence. She stroked my thigh. I settled back on the window sill. Eyes closed, I thought I heard an ocean in my ears. I felt vibration and saw a flash of light. Turning around, I saw a funicular railway running right by the window.

The next day, back on board shooting the breeze, the machinist says, "Hey did you meet crazy Maria?" Ha, I thought. I got there first. Months later, back in New York, talking about Valparaiso with a buddy, out of the blue he asked, "Is crazy Maria still going?"

My final day in Valparaiso, four of us lunched at an upscale businessman's restaurant, the Neptune Bar and Grill. Willy the manager ran a relaxed, refined place serving primarily local business clientele. He changed our money at four times the official rate. We all ordered the shrimp salad, which he promised was very fresh, and washed it down with good Chilean wine. After lunch, we parted company. Two of my companions returned to the ship and Walter Pitman, the Chief Scientist, left for the airport. (More on this lunch at the end of this chapter.)

Having sent my data from the Tahiti-Chile East Pacific transit voyage home with the chief scientist, I planned to hitchhike across South America from Valparaiso to Buenos Aires. Several shipmates gave me a head start by renting a Fiat 600. We spent our first night in the Sheraton Hotel in Santiago. The next day, we drove through the foothills of the Andes up to Portillo, Chile's famous ski area. Portillo is just a few miles from the Argentine border.

My shipmates left me at Portillo. I stepped out on the highway in the morning and caught a ride on a truck going through to Argentina. The road to Argentina turned to dirt just past the ski area. The border crossing was quite interesting. At the time, the route from Chile to Argentina passed through a five-mile-long working railroad tunnel. On certain days of the week, trucks were allowed to use the tunnel, passing one way at a time through the narrow rock passage. There was no formal traffic control, just established hours for each type and direction of traffic. We entered the long tunnel. I held my breath until I knew the light at the end of the tunnel was Argentina, and not an oncoming train or truck.

I left the truck at Plaza de Mulas, about five miles into Argentina. Plaza de Mulas is the jumping off point for the trek into Aconcagua, at 23,000 feet the highest mountain in the Western Hemisphere. While the mountain had been climbed years before, there were not yet expedition outfitters and the walk into Aconcagua was quite remote. Mostly, the Argentine army used the territory for maneuvers.

Approaching Aconcagua from Plaza de Mulas

I backpacked in a full day to a major stream crossing. The elevation was probably about 15,000 feet. I wasn't feeling so hot, so I set up the tent and camped by the stream. Sometime in the night my gut burst. I stumbled out and shat green streams that splashed on the rocks.

I felt strong enough to walk the next morning. The stream was down—the cold night had kept the spring runoff in crystalline form. Easily crossing the stream, I walked up a wide, flat glaciated valley toward the snow line in the distance. After six hours and perhaps a thousand feet in elevation, I reversed course, back toward my camp. The trickling stream of the morning had turned into a torrent of snow runoff. I picked my way carefully across the stream and spent a second night in the valley.

I packed up the next morning and walked back out to the highway. The first ride to come along was a black car with yellow trim, and a taxi light on the roof. The driver, Roberto Arapian drove his taxi in Buenos Aires. He was first generation Armenian, on vacation with his sister, a friend, his sister's friend, and the old Italian shoemaker who lived and worked in the garage in back of his house. They had taken a week-long spring break to drive 800 miles to the Chilean border, then turned around and headed back to Buenos Aires.

In my broken Spanglish, which has not improved much to this day, I explained that I was a taxi driver, too, from New York City. We embraced. Roberto said I was his guest for the return trip to Buenos Aires. That made six of us in the taxicab. The cab ran fine, though the tires went flat on a regular basis, making for many interesting detours day and night in search of mechanics and replacement used tires.

We drove through Mendoza, Argentina's wine country, and across the windswept Pampas, Argentina's cattle country. We camped twice, both nights in wide open spaces by the side of the road. We built a campfire to heat our maté, sipping the hot and sweet liquid through a silver bombilla plunged into a traditional gourd. We told stories in bad Spanish and worse English for hours, and enjoyed the rich stars in a sky that seemed to extend forever.

I stayed with my new friends in Buenos Aires and spent a day with Roberto in his taxi. I rode with him as he picked up fares and passed through the city and its neighborhoods. Roberto and his friends saw me off at the airport.

And that is how I hitched across South America in two rides. And now, about that lunch in Valparaiso. After I returned to the States, I learned that Walter, the chief scientist, had been admitted to the hospital. He stayed there for twenty-eight days and lost a lot of weight. I looked him up after he returned to work and asked him what happened. He said he picked up some food poisoning in Chile and it took that long to get rid of it. I told him about my shitting green and eventually we learned that the other two people at our Valparaiso lunch, who had gone back out to sea, had spent three days in sick bay. So much for that wonderful shrimp salad.

Chapter 13

Driving the Pan American Highway 1972

In 1972, unmoored from my work at sea, restless on land, profoundly, deeply in love, Betsy—the woman who would become the mother of my children—and I spent six months driving from New York through South America. To give the journey a patina of purpose, we incorporated a company, Tierras Imports, to purchase native handicrafts and then resell them in the United States. As the idea matured, we intended to establish commercial relationships with entrepreneurs in market towns in Central America and in the Andes, with the idea that, having become familiar with the handicrafts available in the markets and having established relationships with vendors, we could place orders by telex, pay for them through wire transfer and then market the goods in the U.S. upon receipt. That we actually did some of this astounds me even today.

Charles A. Bookman | **The World Has Changed**

It should surprise no one that Tierras Imports failed. There was a moment when I knew it would fail. Two moments, actually. They both occurred after we had returned from South America. Our first remote order consisted of Aymara pottery, sent from La Paz, Bolivia. The large wooden crate arrived intact at New York's Kennedy Airport. We hired a customs broker and in due course, having cleared customs, the broker arranged for local delivery. One guy with a hand truck unloaded $1000 worth of fragile pottery from his truck. I cringed as he bounced the crate down a short flight of stairs on the way to the freight elevator in my building. Shards rattled inside the crate. The shipment had been okay in Customs. The pottery must have shattered during final delivery.

While the loss of the pottery was financially crippling, the second incident dogged me personally for years. In Panama, Betsy had traveled by small plane to a Cuna Indian village in the San Blas Islands in order to purchase fine molas. Molas are a form of reverse applique embroidery practiced by the Cuna. Cheap molas are sold to tourists in stacks in Panama. The finest molas are worn by the Cuna as blouse decorations. It was these older, finer molas that Betsy had sought by visiting the islands. She returned with a large box of used blouses. Each blouse, front and back, sported an especially fine, museum quality mola.

The molas got hung up in Customs. Expecting to find drugs in our boxes, I think, the disappointed federal officials accused us of smuggling blouses. We maintained that we were not smuggling blouses; we were, in fact, importing art work. The shipment sat. After months of arguing, Customs allowed the shipment in provided we labelled each blouse with a tag identifying it as being made of cotton, which allowed Customs to save face. As for me, I was placed by Customs on a special list of suspected smugglers. For years, whenever entering the U.S., I was pulled aside in the immigration line for additional questioning and more thorough searching.

My notes from our South American journey are hardly exhaustive. I wrote at the time, "Neither of us expected it to be such hard work. Missing sleep, endless chains of chores, for me the car, for Betsy everything else. And there were no days off. She expected more fun and lighthearted moments. I expected more variety."

My notes, edited below, hardly qualify as travelogue but they convey what it is like to make a journey of a lifetime. Re-reading fifty years later, I am amazed that the two of us, in our early twenties, with minimal language skills and little expedition preparation, survived, even thrived along the Pan American Highway. Despite the handicaps and hurdles, the handicrafts picked up along the way paid for my graduate school and for Betsy to finish college. Our relationship survived, even blossomed in the confines of our camper.

In the U.S.

We wanted a pick-up truck with a camper. I found an older pick-up being sold by a construction company. It had an old body but a new engine. Some problems with registration were ironed out by providing a bottle of whiskey to the manager of the New York State licensing office. The camper was magnificent. It had a kitchen, a toilet and a shower. The double bed was situated over the cab of the pickup.

The first rig

Charles A. Bookman | **The World Has Changed**

Our inaugural journey consisted of a drive down New York City's Major Deegan Expressway to our farewell party on an abandoned pier (now today's Chelsea Piers). I was having some difficulty steering because the vehicle swayed from side to side. A state trooper eventually pulled us over. He walked around the vehicle. Leaning in, he shoved the camper. It rocked from side to side on the truck chassis. The trooper said, "I don't know what's wrong with your vehicle but promise me you'll get it off the road and get it fixed." I thanked him.

The farewell party is a blur in my memory, but the diagnosis of our truck is not. The camper was tied down to the truck bed, but where the truck bed was bolted to the truck frame, the bed was completely rusted out. When I felt the camper sway, it was literally shifting free on the truck frame. A welding shop made the needed repair and we set off on our journey.

Crossing the northern tier, we picked cherries in Door County, Wisconsin, and harvested wild rice in Minnesota. We were taken like rubes by carnies at the Northern Wisconsin State Fair in Chippewa Falls. There, we also attended a show by country music star Porter Waggoner, with his sidekick Dolly Parton. Dancing Friday night at a cowboy bar in Montana, we dodged the inevitable barroom brawl. We hit the parks too, Yellowstone and Grand Teton.

While the camper was glamorous it proved ponderous and impractical. The truck got perhaps ten miles to the gallon. We sold it at a used car lot in Salt Lake City, Utah, then purchased an orange and black Volkswagen bus from a guy who had dropped a Chevrolet Corvair engine into it. The engine from that paragon of American auto engineering, the Corvair featured dual carburetors that gave the bus added power. The significance of the dual carburetors was lost on me until I had to clean them of dust and tune them for altitude changes twice a day in the Andes Mountains.

Clocking miles on the interstate, I noticed that the greasy spoon diners were disappearing. New franchise restaurants sprang up almost every day at the highway interchanges. In the space of a single day, we passed Pup'n'Taco, Taco Time, Tico Taco, Taco Bell, Arby's, Lum's Red Barn, Whataburger, Big Beef, Sambo's, Denny's, and Our Dog Parlor. This was food so fast you hardly knew you ate it.

We cruised the California coast from Oregon to the Mexican border. The oil rigs in the Santa Barbara Channel looked to me like gliding water spiders that never moved. Staying with friends in Topanga Canyon, we were told about houses that wash off precipices in flash floods. If the floods don't get you, then the brush fires will (and this was fifty years ago, before widespread awareness of the hazards of changing climate). I was struck with the southern California juxtaposition of lemon trees in the backyard with smog in the face. It was the land of free spirits, Governor Ronald Reagan and the Black Panthers.

Adventures in Mexico

We crossed into Mexico on September 18, 1972 at Nogales, Arizona. Two fifty-cent bribes and we were sailing south through country greener and richer than nearby Arizona. Several hours into Mexico, near Magdalena, little kids sold fresh pomegranates beside the road. Three days later, the pomegranates hatched little fruit flies. Like Charles Lindbergh's stowaway fly, the flies stayed with us for the next thousand miles.

The highway was paved, well-marked, and we felt more or less safe. What caused difficulty was our hankering for adventure. When we entered Mexico, the odometer read 10,000 miles. By the time we pulled into the Panama Canal Zone the odometer was pushing 15,000 miles.

We stayed the first night near Ciudad Obregon, a city reflecting all the new prosperity in Mexico's north. Public investment in water projects seemed to have paid off as the agricultural sector was booming. After eating fine shrimps in a restaurant with a marlin on the wall, we tried our first night camping. The lights were bright, the mosquitoes liked to bite and by 1:30 a.m. we were driving again through the night, trying to outrun the discomfort. It was a wild drive past sugar cane fields. Cattle slept on the highway, trucks roared by, and a violent rain squall flooded the road just before dawn.

We crossed the Tropic of Cancer at 10 a.m. It was marked by a stone obelisk. At lunchtime, we swam in the Pacific Ocean off Mazatlan. In those days, only recently graduated from hitchhiking, I was practiced at sneaking into motel rooms for a quick siesta and perhaps a shower. I was pleased to see that my hitchhiking motel sneaking technique worked as well in Mexico as it did in the U.S.

Half an hour out of Mazatlan two trucks had collided on a bridge across a river. The roadway was completely blocked. One truck hung over the precipice. The other was not quite on the edge. It looked like you could sneak around if you were willing to risk your right front tire hanging nearly over the gorge. There did not seem to be a tow truck anywhere within reach. People were getting ready to spend the night. Not wishing to join them, I squeezed out of my lane. Our narrow VW bus made it past the accident with a hair's breadth to spare. At this point I received my first Mexican driver award from Betsy.

The next day, we went in search of a famous volcano. In 1943, a Tarascan Indian hoeing his cornfield felt the earth start shaking. He ran. The ground ripped open and lava poured out of the fissure. The eruption lasted for nine years. The Paricutin volcano topped out at 9000 feet. Lava engulfed two villages and charred fields for miles. The Tarascans moved a short distance away.

A passable road (meaning there was space to drive between the deep potholes) led to the Tarascan village of Angahuan. The Tarascans produced lacquer bowls, intricately painted. The villagers of Angahuan tapped the pine forests to produce the resin for the lacquer paint.

We rented a guide and horses to visit the volcano. It poured as we galloped down main street then across miserable corn fields spoiled by an over-abundance of ash. Villagers waved as we flashed by. After the corn fields, we descended to the valley

Coming of Age Stories

floor of Paricutin through large pine stands, each tapped by its custodian for resin.

Once on the valley floor, we galloped along the ash plain, moving blindly in the rain, admiring the distant grey shapes wondering when they would take form. Our guide Jose finally reined in, we did likewise. He said look. We looked. There, rising like an idol out of the tangled lava, stood the ruins of the village church, its nave intact. Its steeple had been swept downstream by angry lava. It lay amid sharp basalt boulders at a crazy tilt. The tilted church was all that remained of the Tarascan settlements "before" Paricutin. It is possible to climb down inside the church snaking over and through convolutions of lava to kneel at the altar of Paricutin. It is a shrine now to believers, because it remained undisturbed despite the power and fury of the earth.

On the way out, Jose opened up about Tarascan life. Women marry at thirteen, and have babies at fifteen. Lacquer resin and the volcano are the two main sources of income.

That night we slept at Patzcuaro, a picturesque lakeside village with fantastic markets for pottery dishes, clothing, and wooden boxes made from Jacaranda wood.

Over the next week we drove through central Mexico from Guadalajara to Oaxaca, passing through areas that both Betsy and I had visited before—separately—in 1970. She had spent the summer of 1970 on an archaeology dig in the area that would soon become the Mexican Riviera. I had spent part of the winter driving through Mexico and climbing its big volcanoes.

The province of Chiapas in southern Mexico was new to both of us. Mountainous and remote, it is replete with scenic wonders such as Cañon Sumidero, a 2,500-foot deep limestone gorge at the headwaters of the Rio Grijalva. The Mexican government was constructing a scenic highway along the rim in order to draw tourists to the region. We stopped briefly in San Cristobal de las Casas, a mountain resort town. We found local costumes in abundance, interesting markets, ruins to visit on horseback, and not too many tourists yet.

Central America

We were searched thoroughly at the border when entering Guatemala. Armed military pawed through our motley household goods looking for contraband, or more probably a small payment to encourage them to stop. I was never very good at recognizing and responding to "the touch." Border searches became routine as we crossed international lines on almost a daily or weekly basis.

Nine out of ten Guatemalans are more native than European. We noticed the difference immediately. Even road crews worked in native costume.

We sensed how much more primitive Guatemala was than neighboring Mexico. For one thing, private cars were few and far between in 1972. For another, the main international road, the Pan American Highway was prone to washouts.

We passed through Huehuetenango and then Chichicastenango, with its extensive local market. We hauled up on the shore of Lake Atitlan, which our guidebook, the *South American Handbook* assured us was more beautiful than Italy's Lake Garda. Around this time, the old spirit of adventure came knocking again. It was beautiful, but between the 'Nango towns and the lake, the area attracted other travelers.

We yearned to go deeper, so we charted a course cross country, two days on dirt tracks, to the caves of Lanquin. The caves may be renowned in the annals of speleology, but to me they'll always be the world's greatest swimming hole. Imagine the setting. Two days on a dotted black line on the map. Fording creeks and dodging rockslides at thirteen miles per hour, passing through miles of coffee estates and deep tropical red soil, perfect for bananas and famous highland coffee. On the rainy road, we passed men in native dress carrying machetes, accompanied by their dogs. So many dogs! The women balanced water jugs on their adorned heads. On the afternoon of the second day, we finally entered Lanquin, a town of thirteen thousand, six hours by bus from the district capital of Coban. We enjoyed a delicious chicken dinner for thirty cents, and then hired a guide for the caves.

The caves have been mapped 248 miles underground. The Lanquin river has been followed inside by boat for 48 miles. The view of the entrance is stupendous: a gaping hole in the rock, overhung by red orchids and greenish-gray moss and heavy tropical trees. The river gushes out, aquamarine lime in color and frothy like soda, cool after its underground passage. The water forms a swift pool beneath a leafy branch sagging with orchids. We dove in.

Suitably refreshed and after paying twenty-five cents toward the electric bill, I helped crank the diesel generator. Lights flickered in the cave like fireflies. We followed our teenage guide into a world of white balustrades and buttresses. After an hour walking beside the underground river, the guide slipped behind a rock and killed the lights with a hidden switch. He demanded a second admission fee to turn the lights back on and usher us out of the cave. I would have none of that. Following the sound of his voice, I quickly grabbed him like I meant business. He turned the lights back on and we walked out without further incident.

Five miles by foot further along the river were the natural waters of Semuc Champey. The river had gone underground, leaving fourteen large pools directly above it on the surface. Each has a unique setting and feel. We could have spent days exploring the area.

From Lanquin we retraced our mountainous route in blinding rain to Guatemala City. We found a modest colonial city, modern in parts, with a very nice climate, and where we were robbed for the first time. Little was taken from the car because we owned so little of real value. But we spent comical minutes explaining to the police who were guarding our car that the thief had left the car door open and had not taken anything important because he was going to return for another armful of stuff. If the police would be kind enough to leave, we would stake out the car from the bar across the street and catch the thief red handed. The police agreed, so we staked out the car while the police waited within sight at the corner. The police failed to grasp that we wanted them to leave, on the chance that the thief would return.

We were surprised that we remained healthy despite eating in roadside stands and town marketplaces. Our meals, often soup or stew and tortillas sometimes reeked of pork fat or old cabbage. Worms and flies on produce were common. Other tourists dropped by the wayside while we stormed the gustatory parapet. We felt we were living on borrowed time, but prolonged illness never did plague us.

The *South American Handbook*, a comprehensive guide for business people and overland travelers, was our bible. The guide mentioned we should check in with the parks department in El Salvador, so we did. It was not hard to meet the minister. We simply asked at the front desk of the department. The minister invited us to spend several days at a state run resort on Lake Coatapeque, where the workers all called him "master." One of the minister's minions took us for a motorboat ride on the lake, where we admired green slopes climbing up dormant volcanic cones.

Volcan Ialco, once known as the lighthouse of the Pacific, overlooked the lake. The government had started construction of a large hotel on a subsummit, hoping to harvest the crop of tourists who would come to catch the nighttime displays of volcanic eruptions. However, as soon as they began pouring concrete, the volcano stopped erupting. Even after the hotel had been completed, the volcano remained quiet. The minister of parks was in a quandary about whether or not to open the hotel.

We visited a second volcano, Salvador, with a mile-wide crater 2,500 feet deep. The top is one vast rock garden at 7,000 feet. Local residents raise flowers on its slopes to sell at the market in San Salvador—beautiful carnations, pinks, mums, lilies. Hummingbirds flitted by the dozens from one patch to the next.

We passed Los Auzoles, an acre-wide area of cracked sulfurous hot springs. Mud pots drooled and bubbled, a natural cacophony. The local women, quick to use what they had, washed their laundry in the hot springs. The United Nations (U.N.) harvested here in a different way. The U.N. Development Program had undertaken a pilot project to tap geothermal power. I identified myself as a geothermal scientist from the states and was given a tour of the 80,000-watt power plant. They had drilled into geysers and laid pipe, and now the steam ran through turbines to generate electricity. Both Guatemala and El Salvador shared this power. The project was not large but it was one of the first of its kind.

Next up on the Pan American Highway, Costa Rica. Dubbed "little Switzerland," its small, lovely valleys had been settled by European immigrants. Neat dairy farms dotted the central highlands. What a pleasant diversion after thousands of miles of coffee and banana plantations and primitive huts.

We left the main road to visit a smoking volcano. Where the pavement ended, we stopped at a village to ask directions. "Is it pretty that way?" I asked.

"Silencio" the man at the (horse) tackle store replied. He also mentioned I had to ford two streams. The two turned out to be six, and the streams turned out to be rivers. When our car sank above the axles in white rushing water, I turned back. The volcano would have to wait for another day, or a different traveler.

Another Central American Country, more volcanoes

Near Managua, Nicaragua, we visited a smoking volcano with red hot vents and fresh lava flows. To reach the crater we drove across very recent lava (little plant life as yet), then stopped where the car could climb no further. A swift twenty minute walk up the shoulder through flocks of squawking parrots brought us to the gaping crater. Three hundred fifty feet below, geysers belched sulfurous clouds.. The rock walls were streaked yellow. Wind whistled through gaps in the crater. It was quite a sight.

While Guatemala and El Salvador had been comfortable, perhaps because of their higher altitude, Nicaragua was steamy. Walking off the highway a short way through a cow pasture to swim in Lake Nicaragua, the water was brown and so warm that the swim was not refreshing.

Earlier in the week, we had driven to Rama, the end of the road and gateway to Nicaragua's "Mosquito Coast." A jungle frontier town, mud, babies, mosquitoes, wooden sidewalks. The Bank of Nicaragua was housed in a wooden shack. Rama was sixty miles inland up the Escondido River from the Caribbean. Boats plied downstream to Bluefields, an enclave of English speaking ex-slaves. We had intended to ride downstream but chickened out when we saw the tarantula-infested river craft. We also were not comfortable leaving our Volkswagen bus unattended for days on end in a frontier town at the end of the road.

Finally, we arrived in hot, humid Panama with its "little America," the Canal Zone (this was years before President Jimmy Carter returned the canal to Panama). We had crossed the United States east to west and north to south, and driven the length of Central America. We had been on the road nearly two months, had driven 7,500 miles and spent $2,500. That worked out to three miles to the dollar. At nighttime, I had nightmares of monkey wrenches and spark plugs pursuing me through endless asphalt canyons, blinded by desert suns, choking on thick greenery and our own incomplete combustion. After devastating car repairs and even a complete vehicle switch, we were finally in solid mechanical shape. We had been robbed twice (Guatemala City and San Jose, Costa Rica), so were traveling much lighter with fewer possessions to worry about. Our rear ends were sore from so many hours in the saddle, but we had visited and eaten in Indian markets, swum in underground rivers and climbed live volcanos. We faced a decision, continue on—that involved shipping the bus by boat around Panama's roadless Darien Gap—or heading home to take up a more sedentary and traditional life—together (that part had been settled through the crucible of experiences together on the road). We discussed the options on the veranda of our hotel in Panama City as heavy rains confined us to quarters. There really wasn't much to discuss. To seal the deal, we drove out of Panama City to the very end of the Pan American Highway at the edge of the Darien.

In Panama City, I visited freight agents and arranged for passage to Colombia on the *Rossini*, an Italian Line immigrant ship. We would load the bus onto the boat in Colon, on the Caribbean coast, transit the canal, then sail overnight to Buenaventura, Colombia on the Pacific coast. What adventures awaited on the next leg of our journey?

Driving down the Andes

Five other travelers (in three other cars) booked onto the Italian ocean liner *Rossini*, two Aussies, two Germans, and an Argentine from California. We became chummy while transiting the canal, enough so that in Buenaventura, confronted with a sea of Colombian bureaucracy and outstretched palms, we shared the cost of a "guide" to the paper work. He didn't rip us off too badly. The crux came in the customs office building. One hall, four doors: Secretariat, Sub Administrator, Administrator, and El Jefe. Each with its benevolent grinning occupant, each with outstretched palm. It took a full day to spring the cars.

Despite our successful drive through Central America (only two break-ins), we had heard stories about Colombia. We half-expected banditos around every curve in the road.

It was a hard road into Cali. Our muffler fell off on the way into town. I repaired it using a soup can, a repair I would get very good at in the weeks ahead. Then we ran out of gas. Using our wits, we slept in the van in a wealthy neighborhood where every hacienda had an armed guard.

I spent the next morning in a welding shop repairing the muffler. The proprietor offered me aguardiente at 10 a.m. Betsy went off with the women. I stayed behind backslapping and drinking with the shop owner and his workers. Perhaps this is why the repair took so long and lasted hardly longer than it took.

On the road again later in the day, we drove to Popayan, an old colonial town with a nice museum. We stayed overnight in a hotel, a whitewashed building with exposed beams.

The dirt road south the next day was rough and winding. We leapfrogged with the cars from the boat, part serendipity, part security. Arriving after dark in Pasto, we went to the only restaurant that appeared open. I asked, "Serve supper?"

"No."

"Have meat?"

"Si."

"Rice?"

"Si."

"Beans?"

"Si."

"But no supper?"

"No."

"Well, give me some meat, rice, and beans."

The drive into Ecuador from the Colombia border followed a one-lane cobbled road through deep gorges, over high passes, and along rivers. Near El Angel, the low point (about 5,000 feet) we drove through a village whose genetics must trace back to Africa. Against a backdrop of snow-capped Andes, the village houses were made round, of straw. Dark women wore flashy jewelry.

We arrived at dawn in Otavalo, Ecuador, a wool gathering center. The town is famed for its market, also the colorful costumes of the local folk. The men wear white bell-bottom trousers and carry blue wool ponchos. The women wear red blouses and scads of gold jewelry wrapped about their necks.

The market begins at dawn. By 8 a.m., the wholesale wool merchants had completed their business and left. Throughout the morning, the local merchants continued to sell raw wool, teasels for carding, and hand wool spinners. Food sellers offered fermented blackberry juice, sheep's liver, boar's head, and that finest of Andean delicacies, the cuy, roast guinea pig. While the market ran its course, the women of the town walked along spinning a bobbin in their right hand, carrying the raw wool in their left.

We toured Otavalo with our German friends from the boat, Brigitte and Mike. After the market, we parked outside of town. Brigitte and I strolled up a trail through Indian bean fields to

Coming of Age Stories

11,000 feet while Mike and Betsy entertained the Indians in the village below by teaching them tic tac toe. Up on the mountainside, we noticed the Indians used wooden hoes for cultivating their corn, potatoes, and beans.

Later that day, we passed Cayambe Volcano, 19,000 feet on our way to the equator. At "the line," the government had hammered a brass bar across the road. I crossed it six more times making a lifetime total of 15.

We had an interesting experience right near the equator thanks to a retired U.S. foreign service couple we had met in a restaurant the previous evening. George Walker and his wife Elsie retired to Quito to "take advantage of opportunities." They owned two mushroom caves, a shrimp farm, and a palm oil plantation that sold to Palmolive. George became interested in me after he learned that I had worked in oceanography. He hoped, I think, that I knew something about mariculture and that he might lure me into joining him in opening up shrimp farming along the Ecuadorian coast. With hindsight, I might have been able to fake it, but I am glad that I did not take that road, even despite the mammoth scale that the shrimp industry attained in Ecuador in later years.

George told us to look for a twenty-three bedroom European hunting lodge silhouetted against the mountains when we visited the equatorial monument. There it was, Hacienda Guachala, about a mile due east. We found our way to the eucalyptus-lined drive and then walked into the largely empty house. Just as the equator had been demarcated in the Pan American Highway by a brass rail, a similar brass rail ran across the ornate billiard table. We learned from the caretaker that the lodge used to be the headquarters of the largest cattle ranch in Ecuador. The last owner went to Paris and never came back. After she died, it passed to her five grandchildren. One of them is George Walker's business partner. The estate and grounds were for sale for 20,000 U.S. dollars. Betsy dreamed of buying it and running it as a hotel "right on the equator." Another road not taken. (Wikipedia tells me that Hacienda Guachala is today a hotel, so we were on the right track.)

Charles A. Bookman | **The World Has Changed**

"Recuerdo" from Quito, Ecuador

When not visiting with the Walkers in Quito, I directed my attention to fixing the car. The clutch cable needed to be replaced, and the engine required new plugs and points (remember points?). In between, we visited the cathedral, and conducted business with Ocapa, the national handicraft organization. The gold-covered city cathedral was one of the gaudiest I have ever seen. I watched incredulous as a priest shooed penniless Indios off the front steps like you would clear cobwebs. Evenings, we walked through a local square where I had my shoes shined for pennies. A photographer took our photo with an ancient wooden box camera.

Our car was broken into a third time, in Quito, outside the Walkers' apartment building. There was little left inside, hardly more than our underwear and a spoon, but the VW bus remained a magnet especially since it was so easy to gain entrance by popping open the small front side windows.

The Walkers encouraged us to visit their palm oil plantation on our drive to the coast. We found old, moss covered trees planted in endless rows, festooned with lots of little nuts. As the old trees go out of production, the Walkers replace them with rubber trees.

The drive back up into the Andes from Guayaquil crossed a 10,000-foot mountain shoulder. Somewhere up there, in thick fog, an ocelot crossed directly in front of us. Betsy was dozing, I alone live to tell the tale. Finally, we left the coast behind and burst through the clouds into bright sunshine. Below me were mountainous drops. High above, villagers hoed their small fields. We were back in the Andes.

Our bus with the Corvair engine proved not to be up to the Andes challenge. It had acted up again down on the coast. On the remote road to Salinas, the fan belt slipped off the fly wheel not once, not twice, but twenty-four times. With the slipping fan belt, the engine overheated, eventually charring the engine's exhaust valves. That's not all. The mounting screws for the solenoid (which engages the starter) rattled off. Somewhere in the Andes, they molder in roadside dust. The battery read a charge of zero despite driving all day. The spark plug wires jiggled randomly off the plugs. Despite all, we soldiered on.

After entering Peru, the Pan American Highway hugs the dry coast. We followed slow-moving sugar cane trucks south all day, pulling into a roadside maintenance yard for the night. Sometime after dark, Betsy left the bus to relieve herself. A moment later she cried, "Come help." It was hard to figure out what had happened in the pitch dark, but in the light of our lantern we realized she had sunk up to her thigh into a concrete tank of liquid tar. Fortunately, we carried extra gas, which is an excellent solvent. Later, reeking of petroleum fumes, we salvaged a little slumber.

A cold offshore current keeps the coastline shrouded in mist. Only during rare El Niño years, when the cold current weakens, does it rain. A deluge in a recent El Niño year had turned the mud-walled coastal ruins of the pre-Inca Chan Chan civilization into something that looked like a drip castle on the beach.

The El Niño rains were not the only disaster to plague Peru at that time. A devastating earthquake in May 1970 had shaken the earth for 45 seconds. That may not sound like much, but high in the Andes' Huaraz valley, a gigantic ice block broke loose off Pico Huascaran. The ice block slid into Lake Llanganuco bursting the glacial barrier that held the lake. The resulting lahar buried the valley and towns below killing 70,000 people.

Peru's Huaraz Valley had been known as one of the most beautiful alpine places on earth. We wanted to see it. Prior to the earthquake, a single-track narrow gauge railway connected the high Andean valley with the coastal city of Trujillo. The lahar wiped out the railroad. To help relief efforts, the government bulldozed the mud out of the many tunnels and scraped a primitive track out of the old railroad bed. Asking around in Trujillo, I was told how to find the old tracks, which were upside down. "Just follow them," I was told.

We found the tracks and followed them all day up into the high Andes. At Carhuaz, we entered the fabled Huaraz valley. Two years after the lahar, devastation remained everywhere. The town of Yungay, just below Laguna Llanganuco, remained buried with its inhabitants under 150 feet of debris. In its place stood a primitive iron cross and a collection of khaki Red Cross wall tents.

I felt uncomfortable being a tourist in the midst of such misery. We camped up at the lake, which looked pristine under its snowy patron, Huascaran. How could such a beautiful spot have caused so much devastation?

Continuing on foot, I followed a pack train up toward the high passes on the shoulder of Huascaran. The arrieros (burro handlers) enjoyed the novelty of walking with a gringo. After a second night at the lake, we drove further up the valley. Past the lake and above the lahar, the earthquake had caused considerable damage in the form of collapsed buildings, but it had not caused the total devastation of the lahar, which wiped out and buried everything in its path for a hundred miles.

On the road between Yungay and Huaraz, I heard a sharp noise from beneath the car and suddenly I had no brakes. Fortunately, I was on the valley floor and not negotiating some precarious climb. I coasted to a stop and nursed the car along using manual gearing to brake all the way to a garage in the city of Huaraz. My brake line had snapped and the sudden loss of braking pressure caused a brake shoe to crumple inside the brake drum. In the emergency conditions that still prevailed in Huaraz, I was advised by the military police to hire a truck for the ten-hour transport out of the Andes to Lima. It took a few days to line it all up, but with the assistance of the military officers in charge of the area, that is what we did.

I was fortunate to return to Huaraz forty-seven years later. The drive up from Lima in an express bus still took ten hours. The city itself has been rebuilt and is today a center for treks in the central Andes.

We spent ten days in Lima while the bus was being rebuilt. Our total cash outlay including the car repair and hotel approached 900 dollars. Tapped out, we needed another infusion from our New York bank account. To hurry the car repair and to save a little money, we moved back into the bus while it was still in the garage. Shrugging his shoulders, the owner locked us in the yard along with the junkyard dog who had the run of the place at night. The ploy worked. The car was finished the next day and we headed back into the Andes.

It was December now, and the rainy season had begun. We planned to drive to Cusco via the colonial cities of Huancayo and Ayacucho, a journey of a couple days. Each day would have its 5,000 foot climb over a mountain pass and down the other side. We expected long days, mostly on dirt that would now become mud because of the rains. Landslides would not be far off. We hoped to reach Cusco unscathed.

The road to Huancayo climbs over a 16,000-foot pass. When the sky was clear, we felt like we could reach out and touch the snowy peaks. In La Oroya, a mining center, there was an actual traffic jam, horns honked, cars stalled. What was the cause? A herd of llamas grazing down Main Street. In Huancayo, we dined on a particularly fine pollo a la brasa, Peru's national food fetish—chicken rubbed with garlic, mustard, coriander, and cumin and then grilled.

The highway continued its crazy climbs and descents as it wended toward Ayacucho. In the steepest sections, the roadway occasionally was restricted to one-way traffic. The rainy season continued with daily cloudbursts that turned the road into a sea of mud. We picked up a hitchhiking couple along the way. The man had served with the Peace Corps in El Salvador where he had married a Salvadorean woman. Stopping for lunch in a lonely café, the Peace Corps volunteer excused himself to use the outhouse. While he was gone, our dishes of chicken soup arrived. Each bowl was filled with clear, aromatic broth and one boiled chicken foot. Without exchanging a word, each of us deposited our chicken foot into the bowl of our missing party member. He was delighted when he returned to find such a full bowl of soup.

I remember Ayacucho primarily because I fixed a leaky seal in the transmission housing. Then started the real grind, three days of mud and mountains on the high, primitive road to Cusco. Several times we crossed 14,000-foot passes, then descended 7,000 feet to cross a tributary of the Apurimac River , which flows into the Amazon. At the village of Ocro, the hillside had slid onto the road. Stopped in front of us were a rugged truck and two fully laden buses that had disgorged their passengers, who milled around in the mud. With tire irons and other makeshift tools, we drained the mud to the side of the road. Some of the bus passengers placed nearby rocks into the roadway for traction. After four hours, we had a passable route across the landslide. The Guardia Civil showed up late in the game. The captain asked if we would take photos for the "periodicos."

Driving conditions improved a little the next day, though our progress was complicated by dirt in the fuel line. Parking at a gas station, I removed the fuel tank and drained it, and rinsed it out. We spent that night outside of Cusco at Limatambo.

Cusco is a tourist destination primarily because of the famed nearby ruins of Machu Pichu. Despite its popularity, it deserves its superlative reputation because of its setting, its history, and the vibrancy of a native culture that has survived 500 years of European occupation. The vast public market had many handicrafts of interest to us—alpaca rugs and weavings, lush sweaters for $3.50, exquisite native ponchos. We shopped and bargained and bartered. Betsy found a particularly exquisite woven poncho, crimson and blue and very dusty.

We set off for Machu Picchu in mud and rain. Having traveled so many miles without incident, I suppose an accident was inevitable. When it happened, it wasn't on some remote mountainside, but in the relatively prosperous Urubamba valley where the road rain straight as an arrow. I saw the pick-up truck driving too fast. Both vehicles attempted to stop but skidded instead in the mud. We met head-on at a slow speed. There was little damage to the pickup, no injuries to us worse than a bruise on Betsy's forehead. Our bus sustained a cracked windshield (Betsy's head) and the mashed-up front interfered with the clutch pedal. The other driver asked for compensation. We drove on down to the Guardia Civil outpost in Ollantaytambo. The truck driver became embarrassed asking for damages when he had none. The Guardia decided the accident was due to natural causes, a wet road. We shook hands and parted amicably. A mechanic freed my clutch pedal for $1.75.

Tourists know Ollantaytambo for its impressive Inca ruins and because it is a fine red-tile-roofed town. The Inca fortress rises in back of the modern town. The evening we were there, the government audiovisual truck showed a movie in the town plaza. The truck carried both a generator and a projector. A white building made an excellent screen. The whole town turned out. Dogs and cats, too. The first movie was about British hunting dogs, the second was an interesting propaganda film urging everyone to form coops to control exploitation.

We visited the Inca ruins early in the morning. The ruins rise in a trapezoidal shape up a cliffside. Our guide pointed out to us the execution rock and the altar for human sacrifice. Ollantaytambo held out against Pizarro long enough for the vestal virgin to retreat to Machu Picchu.

The old Inca way goes from Ollantaytambo to Machu Picchu. It was not so traveled in 1972, but today is a major tourist draw. We rode the train down the Urubamba gorge with the other tourists. The Urubamba brawls its way toward the Amazon. While the river looked muddy and especially treacherous, I was told that's its waters are limpid in the April—November dry season and it is well known for outstanding trout fishing.

Our trip along the river was interrupted by a large boulder on the tracks. We waited while a work crew dynamited the boulder and restored the trackway. (The rainy season wreaks havoc in innumerable ways.)

Arriving late at the Aguas Calientes station 1,200 feet directly below Machu Pichu, we eschewed the local bus and climbed the steep trail up to the ruins. It took a long, sweaty hour with our heavy backpacks. I enjoyed stretching my legs in the jungle foliage; Betsy not so much.

The well-known ruins fit the scenery perfectly. Machu Pichu sits in a saddle between two peaks, Machu and Huayna Pichu. The Urubamba gorge surrounds the ruins on three sides. The great buttress of sheer rock drops down 1,200 feet to the river. Green crags rise up in nested tangles on all sides, giving way to great snowy mountains that rise even higher. The setting is truly a site to behold.

The next morning, I followed the old Inca Trail in mist at dawn as it climbed along the spine of the buttress back toward the gate of the sun. I marveled at the views of the snowy mountains. The ruins beckoned far below. When you don't have horses and you don't have the wheel, building a road is a much simpler task. The Inca way is 4 feet wide and uses many steps. Paved with large stones, it is still in fair repair.

Machu Picchu was no ordinary farming center. Fully half the town was devoted to religious activities. The stone work in the ceremonial areas is very fine. Corn grew on terraces of filled earth. We sat high up on burial rock, where the good photos are shot, and watched the late afternoon light play games on the rocks and moss. We camped that night below the Machu Pichu hotel in the rain.

From Cusco, we stayed high on the road to La Paz, at 11,000 feet the highest international capital in the world. Our route took

Coming of Age Stories

us along the shore of Lake Titicaca and through the small city of Puno.

We rolled through the small town of Sicuani on a Sunday afternoon. The streets were filled with a communist-led demonstration against the government. When we arrived, the demonstration turned into an anti-American rally with shouts of "gringo go home" and "bajo con yanquis," and speakers pointing us out from the platform, all of which we took in good-natured stride. While the affair struck me as more of a Sunday band concert in the park than a political movement, I sensed deep social unrest. Not many years later, the area we had traversed since we left Lima became the center of the Maoist uprising known as the Shining Path. In my notes I wrote, " I take heart in the fact that the campesinos actually realize that they have little to lose and when you've got nothing, you've got nothing to lose. Changes are coming. They may be undirected right now, but there will be a path forward to fundamental change."

Given the many travails with the car, we decided that when we entered Bolivia, we would do whatever it took to avoid posting a bond for the car (posting a bond by means of a *carnet de passage* obtained through the American Automobile Association was standard practice at the time). Without a bond, we could sell the car, which had become a liability. In the end, the border officials allowed us to bring the car in without posting a bond. The process took four hours and a private visit with the office director.

We settled into La Paz determined to sell the car and our few remaining possessions. I placed a small notice in the local paper. In the end, the car went without papers to someone who hoped to use it for a collective taxi, or possibly to run drugs across the border into Brazil. We didn't know and we didn't care, as we counted his 25,000 greasy Bolivian soles (500 U.S. dollars). The rest of our stuff, mainly our camping kit and excess clothes we unloaded in a sidewalk sale in front of our hotel. From La Paz, Bolivia to Argentine Patagonia, we would travel as tourists.

La Paz, Bolivia is second only to Kabul, Afghanistan in its physical isolation from other world capitals. The country is land-locked and the air is thin because of the altitude. Roads are abysmal and rail lines few and far between. The city itself has more steep grades than San Francisco. In the downtown, there's only one street you can call level. All others careen around or over. The few sidewalks typically have handrails. Even new streets are paved with cobblestones because it is cheaper to pay the labor than to bring the cement up by rail from Chile. The wealthy live near the city center, at lower altitudes where there's more oxygen. The poor live on the high slopes that top out about 13,000 feet.

I wanted to get to the bottom of some family history in La Paz. In the 1950s, my Uncle Joseph Schrank (my mother's brother) traded penny stocks on Wall Street. He followed a Bolivian gold mining company, Bol Inca. Everyone in my mother's family owned a few shares. The annual corporate reports read as though the big strike was just around the corner, but the penny stock never seemed to make it out of the basement.

I visited the gold mining regulator at the Ministry of Mines, Humberto Fernandez. He knew Bol Inca very well. He shared a fond memory of drinking beer on a river boat with Ralph O'Neill, the company president. Mr. Fernandez told me that Bol Inca was formally dissolved a little over a year before when it and its parent company, Tidewater Oil, renounced all mineral rights. He showed me on a map where the holdings were, near Ciudad Guanay northeast of La Paz. The mineral rights fanned out along several rivers, the Mariri, Kake, Zongo, and Coroico.

Bol Inca failed for lack of common sense. Another mining company was making money off the gold sands of the same river. The other company employed a dredge with a sixty cubic-foot bucket. Bol Inca had purchased a much smaller dredge, one with a fifteen cubic foot bucket. It cost quite a lot to ship the smaller dredge from the Yukon River to the Bolivian jungle. The cost of mobilization and the size of the dredge apparently made the difference between bankruptcy and profit. Bol Inca's dredge remained in the jungle, half in packing crates, half out, and the mineral rights were once again up for grabs. So much for gold and the stuff of dreams.

Coming of Age Stories

Christmas in La Paz felt a little like Halloween. For days, kids in Inca costumes had been running around downtown making music with drums, harmonicas, and pan pipes, and asking for hand-outs. Santa Claus made an appearance; this was very welcome after our stay in Peru where Papa Noel was branded a political enemy. In contrast to somber Peru, we found Bolivia very festive. Music flowed through the streets, people wore colorful costumes, and there was plenty of alcohol and joyful noise.

After La Paz, traveling as tourists, we visited Paraguay in order to see Iguazu Falls, then traveled on to Buenos Aires, Argentina. From Buenos Aires, we flew to Ushuaia, Argentina at the foot of the continent. We walked to the shore of Cape Horn at Lapataia Bay. From that southernmost point of the continent, we stared out at the Southern Ocean.

In Patagonia

We visited Rio Gallegos, Patagonia's main port, on our return journey. From there we rode a rough local bus five hours across Patagonia to see the Petito Moreno glacier, which rises in the Andes. After Rio Gallegos, we flew to Punta Delgada, a national park known for abundant sea life. Arriving late in the afternoon, we hired a taxi to drive us out to see the sea elephants and the penguins. At the time, there were no regulations or controls. We walked right out into the sea elephants and played up close and personal with the penguins. Knowing today how easy it is to permanently harm wildlife by disturbing them, I would never do that again, but the experience at the time was magical. So magical in fact that our visit was graced with a magnificent rainbow that I captured in a photograph. Penguins and rainbows, oh my!

That has been the story of our South American adventure in a 1963 Volkswagen bus with a Chevrolet Corvair engine. As I noted at the beginning of this narrative, we worked harder than we ever had, spending eight to twelve hours a day in the saddle. We confronted roadblocks figuratively and literally at every turn. What did we learn on the road trip of a lifetime? I became an ace roadside mechanic. We picked up some good stories. We survived as much time together, we figured, as the average couple spent in five years (most of it without a functioning car radio). We were somewhat happier for the journey and certainly a lot wiser. We sank about 3,500 dollars into Tierras Imports Inc., our handicraft firm; the business paid for a year of college and graduate school. Other than our shared experience that deepened our love, we were left with out-of-date business cards and stationery, and a few unsold handicrafts like molas and pottery. We experienced marvelous scenery and gained rudimentary Spanish, enough to carry on basic conversations. Would I do it again? Absolutely (same goes for our twenty-year marriage).

Chapter 14

More Roots and Branches

As we near the end of the story, there is more to tell in order to fully understand how the seeds I planted in my youth blossomed into great loves and friendships; how side notes of youthful exploration matured into the wisdom of experience. This chapter presents branches of experience—my youthful adventures in love and lust; my irrational, almost adoring attachment to inanimate objects, notably cars; an entrepreneurial story from my year in Rhode Island; and the beginnings of my love affair with the concertina and playing music for old-time dancing. These roots and branches of my life—and the friends I made along the way—have made it all worthwhile.

Adventures in Love and Lust (1966-1971)

Everyone has awkward self-discovery stories. My memories of early romantic adventures involve the outdoors. Perhaps that is normal when you don't have a place of your own, I don't know.

I look back on these early experiences with amusement and great fondness. I hope my partners, who shall remain nameless, share fond memories as well.

Life on the Housatonic. Wandering off from our high school camping trip on the banks of the Housatonic, we came upon a camping trailer on a secluded stretch of river. The door was unlocked. Entering, we snuggled together on the neatly made bed. As the British say, we snogged, seemingly for hours. When dusk finally approached, we pulled ourselves apart, bade goodbye to our little Eden, and returned to our group camp.

Fishing the river the following morning, I drank great drafts of the mighty Housatonic. I felt on top of the world, with that unabashed afternoon romance foremost in my mind. Twelve hours later, I was doubled over in pain, heaving a total of sixteen times over a very sleepless night.

It seems, while snogging, we had missed the warning not to drink the Housatonic as in those days it carried effluent from nearby paper mills and municipalities. I would like to tell you, dear reader, that I learned something on that camping trip about the sweet pain of love, but I would still, in a New York minute, sneak away from the crowd with a partner, warnings be damned.

Learning to Paddle Your Own Canoe. I became intimately acquainted on our high school senior trip with Lake George in New York's Adirondack Mountains. In May, with the ice mostly (but not entirely) melted, we paddled our canoes toward an island in the middle of the lake. I shared my canoe with my sweetie of the moment, a smart and sassy young woman, but a mere slip of a thing. Somewhere in the middle of that big lake, the wind came up and swamped us. We found ourselves splashing in 38 degree water. My girlfriend was so thin, I thought she was going to go hypothermic any second. Just in time, a Chris Craft came to our rescue. The skipper and his wife lowered a ladder and pulled us out of the water. They ordered us to take off our sopping clothes and climb into their double bed, then plied us with

Coming of Age Stories

tumblers of scotch. Soon, warmed up snuggling together naked in bed with drinks, we were in high school heaven! We stayed in bed together while our rescuers cruised the lake looking for an islet overrun with high school kids. A good time was had by all. Much later, my dear girlfriend told me that henceforth I would have to paddle my own canoe.

New York Dates. My freshman quarters at Columbia were in what was called a quad suite, two double rooms sharing a bathroom. A suite mate from Bethesda, MD fancied himself a card shark. He hosted a running poker game where the stakes sometimes reached hundreds of dollars. He seemed always to win and towards the end of the semester he had enough disposable cash that he was hiring limousines for his date nights.[1]

In a hurry to meet people of the opposite sex, I joined an early version of a dating service. Naturally and obviously, they matched the Jewish boy from Columbia with the Jewish girl at Barnard. She was nice enough, but there was one problem. She lived with her parents in outer Brooklyn, a walk from the New Lots subway. (For my non-New Yorker readers, the ride from Columbia to New Lots takes an hour and a half, longer if you have to wait for a train in the middle of the night.) One date where I picked her up and dropped her off at her home was enough to cure me.[2]

Another early long distance (for New York) relationship involved a woman I met while rock climbing. She lived on Staten Island. Fortunately, I had a car by this time but a couple of late-night trips across the Verrazano Bridge encouraged me to look closer to home.

---

[1] Years later, he told me that he had learned card mechanics, which he would employ one or two hands each evening. His ill-gotten winnings came mostly from wealthy Middle Eastern students who were oblivious to his hand-fixing, and who could absorb the substantial losses.

[2] The woman in this paragraph emigrated to Oregon after the Columbia Uprising of 1968. In a curious twist, she crossed the country with a friend as both were headed to Reed College and somehow found each other, perhaps through a "Rides Wanted" bulletin board.

I have spun other tales of love and lust elsewhere in this manuscript. They include flings with Pueblo girls in New Mexico, with Hippie girls along California's Big Sur coast, and brief encounters in ports in Latin America and Africa. I suppose my early encounters don't measure up to today's correct behavior where partners communicate directly and supportively every step of the way. I get it and I want to thank every young woman who helped me find my way even if my journey falls short of today's standards. Judge not lest ye be judged.

Farewell Argentina (don't cry for me)

Car Stories, 1967—

The Beach Boys sang about the "Little Deuce Coupe" in 1963. The "Deuce," a 1932 Ford with a flathead V-8 engine, was a popular drag racer. Hot Rod Rock was real California kitsch. While my first car felt like a little deuce coupe to me, the Beach Boys would have considered it the exact opposite. Flush with my first paycheck from the US Forest Service in the summer of 1967 and tired of hitchhiking to my remote duty post at the edge of New Mexico's Pecos Wilderness, I thumbed my way to a used car lot in Albuquerque where I fell for a pasty-colored 1956 Nash Rambler for which the dealer asked fifty dollars. Everything was a little off with the car. The front fender careened at an angle. A hink prevented the steering wheel from gravitating back to neutral position, probably from the same accident that disoriented the front fender. The turn signals blinked only occasionally. The driver-side window sometimes refused to crank.

Getting the jalopy off the lot presented challenges. Starting the car and looking at the engine, I noticed a fuel leak. The dealer ordered his mechanic to tighten the fuel line. The brakes were in dire condition and the tires if not bald were poor quality retreads. The dealer said, take it or leave it. I would be on my own with those.

That car meant freedom. I could work in the woods and on weekends make and meet new friends in Santa Fe and Taos. I soon learned that the hinky steering meant I could take my hands off the wheel on straightaways. I even wrote a postcard or two while driving.

Beginning with the Nash Rambler, there has always been a used car or at least an old car in my life. The most recent was my Toyota Camry, which I bought new in 1998. It was still my "new car" when we drove it the length of the Pacific Coast in 2003. It was going strong a decade later, when in a single season we drove from Seattle to Cabo San Lucas at the southern tip of Baja California, and then later in the year from our home in Seattle to Anchorage, Alaska. These wonderful road trips generated their own stories, so I won't describe them further other than to encourage you to read them as well.[1] After years of dedicated service, the Camry became the designated second car in my life. Even with its cracked windshield, malfunctioning driver-side window, roof leak requiring bailing after heavy rains with a turkey baster ,and dented rear fender, it held pride of place at the curb in front of my house until 2024.

My first new car was an egg-shaped 1969 Saab. I bought it from a dealer in Wappinger's Falls, New York. Less than a day later I got stuck in traffic at night on the Cross Bronx Expressway. After half an hour and about a half-mile of progress, I noticed the gas gauge was low. I exited at Tremont Ave.

---

[1] Tales from these journeys will appear in volume two of my memoirs.

Charles A. Bookman | **The World Has Changed**

The neighborhood was sketchy then. For all I know, it's still sketchy today. I Filled the car, paid, then climbed back in and cranked the starter. The engine compartment burst into flames. The gas station owner ran out with a fire extinguisher and sprayed CO_2 all over the engine compartment. He put the fire out, but the fire had melted the wires and hoses in the engine compartment, and the chemicals from the extinguisher had gotten sucked into the engine. My less-than-one-day-old new car was a mess.

I called the dealer to tell him what had happened. He said, "Why are you calling me? What do you want me to do about it?"

"Fix it," I said.

He took a week to pick up the car from the gas station. He refused to pay storage charges, and took six weeks to fix the car. Then, he refused to release the car until he had been reimbursed for the warranty work by the regional distributor.

I lost patience. I recruited my bulkiest, most buff friend for a recovery expedition. We drove up to the dealership in a borrowed car. We walked into the manager's office. My friend, who stood about 6'4" and filled the entire door frame said, "We're not leaving without the car." The manager turned over the keys.

I replaced the Saab with a new Dodge van in 1973. That was before "Quality was Job One." The standard warranty in that banner year for Detroit was twelve months or 12,000 miles, whichever came first.

I was in graduate school in Rhode island at the time. After a long, dreary New England winter, with spring break on the horizon, my girlfriend and I set our sights on the Florida Keys. We brought along a friend and our two dogs, and strapped my aluminum canoe to the roof. Somewhere on the drive South, the odometer turned over 12,000 miles. Seemingly within minutes of that milestone, the car began to smoke. By the time the odometer reached 12,500, I was adding two quarts of oil to the engine at every fill-up. Doing a rough calculation, I could see that the odometer would read over 14,000 miles before we returned to Rhode Island.

I asked gas station attendants what they thought I should do (remember when there were gas station attendants?). The responses ranged from faggedahaboudit oil is cheap to tough luck you'll have to put in a replacement engine. Desperate by the time we reached New York City, I found the man with the plan at the final fill-up. This guy, somewhere in the Bronx, looked me in the eye and said, "Don't chance it. Go to the hardware, buy yourself an electric drill. Unhook the odometer cable where it goes into the transmission. Put the end of the cable in the drill bit and plug the drill in."

He was right. The drill reversed the odometer at the rate of about 150 miles per hour and about ten hours later my car was within warranty again. I drove it into the dealer. No questions were asked. He gave me a quart of dyed, test oil, asked me to drive around and come back on the day when the regional rep was in. I did as he asked and I got a ring job for free. The car worked fine for the next eight years. Fifty years later, I still have the drill, use it all the time.

I had a 25-yr love affair with this car, and this woman. We drove to the tip of Baja and to Anchorage in 2014

There are so many car stories. I bought an Audi station wagon at an auto auction. (Note: auto auctions can be habit forming and are almost always a bad idea.) This particular Audi needed a new front end. While that doubled my investment in the car, the car started and stopped on cue. It was on its way, I thought, to becoming reliable transportation. That is, until the rear seat burst into flame under my teenage sons, who were admittedly horsing around. I wasn't going all that fast as they bailed out of the flaming vehicle like Hollywood stunt men. As I pulled over to the road shoulder, I watched dumbfounded as my boys expertly tucked and rolled to extinguish the flames.

Why had the rear seat blown up into a fireball? I studied the car manual. It turns out the battery is under the seat. A little plastic thingy that looks like a bottlecap keeps the "hot" battery terminal from shorting out on the rear seat springs. Of course, by the time a car reaches the regional auto auction, the likelihood of the plastic doohickey being where it is supposed to be is miniscule. I wrote to Audi explaining the flaw and the liability that went with it. They could've cared less. They responded with an obnoxiously annoying kiss-off letter denying all responsibility. I scavenged a new rear seat from a junkyard and even found a replacement doohickey.

These stories feed the endless debate about which is better, an old car or a new car. While the debate may never be settled, I patronized a mechanic once who understood the arguments better than most. After I complained to him about my frequent visits and the high cost of his repairs, he said, "Look at it this way. You can buy a new car and pay the bank a couple of hundred a month, or you can keep your heap and pay me a couple of hundred a month. With the bank, you support faceless capitalism. With me, you know you will always get a warm handshake and a good story."

Daddy's Bread: A Rhode Island Origin Story, 1973-1974

It was put up or shut up time. After working three years as a sea-going oceanographic technician, the writing on the proverbial wall became clear. Apply to graduate school in geophysics, or move on. I struggled with the decision. More inductive in my thinking than analytical, math never came naturally. I was inter-

Coming of Age Stories

ested in the geography of the oceans more than in understanding how they came to be, even though my work, which helped confirm the theory of plate tectonics, was all about their (and the continents') origins.

Clarity dawned in June, 1972, while I worked aboard the French oceanographic vessel, the *Jean Charcot*. I had seen an advertisement on a bulletin board at my home institution, Lamont Geological Observatory (now Lamont-Doherty Earth Observatory) about a marine policy degree program at the University of Rhode Island (URI) and had sent for a pamphlet, which had found its way into my luggage. The Law of the Sea was being negotiated at the United Nations at the time. Applying to URI for the 1973-74 academic year, I imagined myself an ocean diplomat.

Louis Alexander, former U.S. State department Geographer and the program director, was encouraging about paid work on campus to provide some income while working toward my degree. Of course, when I showed up, he said he had never said anything of the kind. That left us scrambling for money throughout the year. Betsy waited on tables, cleaned houses, and packed crab meat at Point Judith. I did occasional odd jobs, such as lawn care, and we drew my paltry savings down to zero (my grandfather had died that Spring and left me 5,000 dollars).

Our largest expense was of course our house, a modest farm house on Moonstone Beach Rd., less than a mile from the ocean. Our rent was $200 per month, with the expectation that we would vacate by Memorial Day so that our landlord, an anthropology professor at Brown University, could use the place during the summer.

Moonstone Beach turned out to be, in season, a nude beach heavily favored by New England gays. Perhaps it still is. The dunes between the beach and the salt ponds provide nesting habitat for the piping plover and a lot more shenanigans besides.

The house was surrounded by potato fields, which we gleaned right after the mechanical harvest. We stored hundreds of pounds of potatoes in the basement. The potatoes, supplemented with mussels harvested from the salt marshes, fish parts taken from the cannery, and leftovers from Betsy's restaurant work, constituted the majority of our diet throughout the year.

The Hopkins family lived next door on a property that had been in the family for generations. Everett, the patriarch, a school principal, for extra income harvested watercress from the tidal creek that flowed in back. He sold the watercress from a rusty refrigerator that constituted his roadside stand. The refrigerator sat adjacent to our property. Across the road, at the intersection of Moonstone Beach Road. and Matunuck Schoolhouse Road, Everett rented a collection of beach shacks in the summertime for unconscionable prices.

The Hopkins kids ranged in age from pre-school to late teenage. Our favorite was five-year-old Jenny who showed up on our doorstep one day with a dead bird in her pocket. She introduced us to the rest of her family, and through Jenny we got to know our neighbors.

As winter turned into spring, we grew desperate for funds. When we finally ran short of potatoes, Betsy started baking bread for our starch mainstay. A favorite recipe was Anadama, made with cornmeal and molasses. She also occasionally baked quick breads, such as banana loaf.

We bumped into Everett one day. We talked about our financial plight as it was very much on our minds. On the spur of the moment, Betsy asked Everett if he would mind if we placed a few loaves of bread in his refrigerator stand. He said, "No problem."

Word of the fresh breads being sold alongside the watercress spread quickly through the university and the local communities. By the time the tourists showed up in late May, Betsy was baking hours a day and loaves were flying off the refrigerator shelves. She kept on baking and we lived on the proceeds until we finally moved to Annapolis, Maryland at the end of July.

Always the entrepreneur, Everett took over the baking once we left. He started selling to restaurants and specialty stores throughout Rhode Island and eventually paused his school administrator career, devoting all of his effort to "Daddy's Bread."

The business has waxed and waned over the years. At times, it was the major artisan bread in Rhode Island. For many years, it has been a profitable and much valued way station near the beaches of South Kingstown, Rhode Island. It is headquartered today in those rustic beach shacks across the road. More recently, it has returned to its seasonal roots beloved all over the area and by the beach goers as well. I understand the business is in the care now of daughter Jenny Hopkins, she of the little dead bird fame. http://www.daddysbreadri.com/

The potato fields sprout houses now, not tubers. The dunes are protected for the piping plovers; there are fewer gay nude sun worshippers and shenanigans in the dunes. Our old green farmhouse sports white siding now. Watercress still grows in the tidal stream out back, and the air has the salt tang of the sea. I long to return to Moonstone Beach, preferably in September, when the ocean is at its warmest, and the bread still comes daily out of Daddy's oven.

When the Raccoon Fell Through the Roof: Musical Beginnings (1962-1979)

True confessions. The first time I played music in public, I was "volunteered" to accompany hymns on the piano at boarding school Sunday service. I can still pound out "Old Hundredth" ("Praise God, from whom all blessings flow") when called upon. The performance must not have been too awful because occasionally an upper class woman with a beautiful soprano voice would join me for a brief recital, a choral duet of Handel or some such. Our ecumenical interludes were mercifully cut short when the school headmaster died unexpectedly. Sunday services were suspended and never restarted.

On my sail training ventures, I brought a harmonica. Straddling the bowsprit, I would blow folk tunes learned at summer camp, like the *Titanic* folk song ("It was sad when that great ship went down"), *The Sloop John B* ("Hoist up the John B's Sails, See how the mainsail sets..."), and Hudie Ledbetter's theme, *Good-*

night Irene. The harmonica notes would dissipate quickly in the ocean breezes, so my shipmates never seemed too disturbed.

Since making music had become part of my life, naturally when Betsy and I planned our South American adventure (chapter 13), I wanted to bring some musical entertainment along. Where others might have made sure the car radio worked (which it didn't), I purchased a push-me/pull-you concertina at a music store on New York's lower East Side. It would be years before I learned that kind of diatonic instrument was called an Irish concertina.

I enjoyed playing my harmonica tunes on the concertina until the concertina was taken from our Volkswagen bus in the first of three car robberies, in Guatemala City. Oh well, easy come, easy go. Perhaps somewhere in Guatemala, someone is making sweet music on my old concertina.

When exactly in 1973 or 1974 I purchased another concertina, I don't recall. The second time around I purchased a fully chromatic instrument, called an English concertina. It was modern, Italian-made. I was still playing it when I joined the Peascods Gathering open band in Washington, D.C., in 1977. I still own it.[1]

Many a summer evening, I played that concertina on the front porch of our little farmhouse in Harwood, Maryland. As I grew more proficient, I joined other musician friends, notably Jean Becker, who lived in Baltimore and played autoharp, and Paul Miller, who worked with me at the Maryland Department of Natural Resources and played guitar. Jean and Paul knew each other from graduate school at Johns Hopkins University.

One of my musician friends must have mentioned a dance music workshop in Baltimore with the English dancing master Marshall Baron. This would have been in the Spring of 1977, shortly before Tyras was born. I am not sure what propelled me, but I drove up to Baltimore for the day-long workshop. Such a small, inconsequential decision altered the direction of my mu-

---

[1] For descriptions of my concertinas, see https://bookmansopinions.blogspot.com/2018/12/concertinas-i-have-known.html

sical life. There were perhaps fifteen musicians at the workshop. My friends Jean and Paul didn't show, so I didn't know a soul in the room as we struggled for an hour through the fast-paced reel, *Mason's Apron*, which still, to this day, I can't play well.

Four dance musicians came from Washington, D.C.: Dick Atlee, Chris Hough, Carl Minkus and Lorraine Molofsky. They had started playing together twice a month at the regular English country dance of the Folklore Society of Greater Washington. They formed the core of a fledgling open band that did not yet have a name. Over lunch they encouraged me to join their practices, which I did.

The open band started when several musicians who regularly attended the monthly English country dances of the folklore society started supplementing the usual recorded music with their own enthusiastic if not very polished performances. The dancers preferred the recorded music because it was more dependable (the musicians didn't melt down mid-tune, bringing the dance to a halt). Unfortunately, one evening the caller's car was broken into and his record collection was stolen. That left the dancers with no alternative but to rely on the open band performers. Dick Atlee, who had worked at a folk music camp, took the responsibility seriously. He began to assemble a collection of jigs, reels, waltzes and other tunes that eventually grew to fill two notebooks.[1]

I joined the band at that moment, when the Washington, DC folk dancers, of necessity, relied on the band for their music. We needed a name and in desperation twisted the title of the well-known Morris dance tune *Gathering Peascods* into "Peascods Gathering." The core of the band consisted of a large handful of local musicians. Dick Atlee, impresario and organizer extraordinaire, played accordion, but Peascods was also blessed with a plethora of talented accordionists. Chris Hough was a dedicated

---

[1] Dick Atlee's xerox collection of folk dance tunes spread far and wide. After I moved to Seattle in 2000, I encountered versions of it on the west coast.

dancer and talented accordion player. In the 1980s, Fred Aalto, a Central Intelligence Agency linguist and musicologist provided a third accordion. Carl "Have marimba will travel" Minkus was the band's intrepid percussionist. When not making music, Carl translated Russian and Chinese scientific works for the Congressional Research Service. Faith Coddington from Potomac played an astounding bluegrass-style fiddle. Joining on fiddle was Bob Holloway who taught music in the Prince George's County school system. Lorraine Molofsky had contra danced at Cornell and joined the band soon after she moved to Washington, D.C. to work on children's nutrition programs. Lorraine mostly played recorder, but she enjoyed subbing on washtub base and even trotted out her saxophone from time to time.

We had a harder time keeping guitarists, perhaps because playing guitar for dancing is all about keeping the rhythm, usually with the basic three-chord progression (like G, D,C). Not too challenging for an accomplished guitarist. Earl Williams, an extremely versatile musician was our stalwart guitarist in the early days. Not too long after I joined the band, Joel Edelman showed up—and almost forty years later, he still provides the guitar rhythm for the Peascods. Joel is a stoic if there ever was one.

These fine musicians formed the core of the band. Since Peascods was an open band, anyone could come to practice and play at the dances. Serious musicians, like the harpist who won a national competition, or the song writing couple that composed beautiful ballads, came and went as they sought different challenges.

In its heyday in the 1980s, Peascods fielded more than twenty musicians, including three accordions, three guitars, five fiddles, two concertinas, recorders and flutes, a harp, dulcimers and a washtub base. Forty years later, a version of Peascods Gathering continues to play for the country dances of the Folklore Society of Greater Washington.

Because Peascods would play anywhere and usually for free, it was only natural that the enterprising park ranger responsible for the transformation of the Glen Echo amusement park to a national heritage facility asked the band to play for contra dances in the old Spanish Ballroom.

Today's thriving Glen Echo Park Arts and Cultural Center on the banks of the Potomac River on the western edge of Washington, D.C., is supported by a foundation and owned by the National Park Service. Several nights a week, hundreds of dancers flock to the refurbished Spanish Ballroom for swing, ballroom and contra dances. Glen Echo in the 1970s was an abandoned, dilapidated amusement park in search of a mission. Buffeted by the trials of integration and eventually urban race riots, and especially the 1960 abandonment of the trolley line that brought summer crowds, the old amusement park closed in 1968. The rides were dismantled in 1971 and coincident with the park's listing on the National Register of Historical Places, the National Park Service took over the park grounds. Activating the Spanish Ballroom with dances was one of the earliest cultural activities started by the Park Service. This was largely due to the personal enthusiasm of the original ranger, Diane Kellogg, a resident of nearby Cabin John, Maryland.

Through Diane's good offices and hard work, Peascods Gathering began a forty-year tradition of contra dancing in the Spanish Ballroom. The Spanish Ballroom dated from the park's heyday in the 1920s and 1930s. By the time we played there, the walls had decayed, the roof had gaping holes, the lighting was poor, and heating and air conditioning were non-existent. Yet the ballroom still had a magnificent hardwood floor. When a hundred dancers stomped their feet in unison, the building shook. One hot and humid summer evening, while we played a particularly rousing tune the dancers stomped and the building shook so hard a raccoon tumbled out of a gaping hole in the ceiling. Rocky landed smack in the middle of a contra line. Shaken but not bowed, he scooted off into the shadows. The dancers didn't miss a beat.

As Glen Echo became more established, enthusiastic local philanthropists endowed a foundation to support arts at the center. One by one, the buildings were restored. While Peascods was relegated to the shadows, we band members took special pride in having helped launch dances that continue to play an important part in Washington, D.C.'s cultural life.

As our musicianship grew, so did the opportunities to play. We bought a sound system and established a bank account for the perpetuation of the band, not for the enrichment of any band member. With the proceeds of our dances, we added to our equipment and occasionally brought in more experienced musicians to share their experience with us.

In 1978 and 1979, we played all-night country dances outside of Harpers Ferry, Virginia. The organizers turned to Peascods because we had so many musicians that we could play nonstop all night long, with one musician stepping in when another needed a break. Also, we played for free.

From the Washington Post (1979)

Enthusiastic dancers are enthusiastic about all night dances. After many hours of stepping in time to the music, the dancers become high on the music and dance. That is, until they drop from exhaustion in the wee hours. By 4 a.m. at the 1979 all-night dance, there seemed to be more musicians than dancers. Carl, our elfin percussionist, knew just what to do. Heading into the night towards his car, he returned with a snare drum. Striking the drum head loudly with his sticks, he rata-tat-tatted out the opening rhythm of "Marching Through Georgia." Once the rest of us joined in, you could hear our rendition of the sprightly Civil War anthem all the way across the river in Harpers Ferry. Dancers who had drifted off woke up with a start. Soon, they came back to the dance floor and by 5 a.m. a hundred or more dancers stomped until the sun rose and breakfast was served.

Fifty years later, I still play the concertina on my porch. With Peascods, I learned how to play in an ensemble, how to pick up tunes by ear in a group, and how to keep the rhythm even when the tune otherwise gets away from me. The members of the band are lifelong friends. I suppose we will play at each other's funeral, until, like at the all-night dance, there is no one left to play for. Then maybe I will hear the incessant strains of "Marching Through Georgia."

Halloween Friends 1968—2000s

It started in the 1960s and didn't peter out until the millennium—nearly forty years of unseasonable antics in the Adirondack mountains of my youth. At the height of the Blueberry Marching and Chowder Society celebrations, upwards of thirty old and new friends gathered annually at the end of October on the side of Mount Marcy (New York State's high point). We'd spend a freezing, wet night downing a case of Veuve Clicquot champagne and dining on Kentucky Burgoo heated over a camp stove. The pumpkin ceremony was the height of the evening. A large pumpkin was opened and cleaned out, then filled with apple cider and candy corn, and passed from frozen hand to frozen hand. When it was your turn, you offered a benediction to the great pumpkin, the mountains and your comrades. Then you lifted the pumpkin to your mouth, swigged the vile swill, and passed the pumpkin on to the next gullible soul. The following morning, hung over, drenched, and frozen, those who were able carried the pumpkin the rest of the way to the summit. Lighting a candle in the wind and sleet, we left our offering to the mountain gods.

How did this begin? Several summer hiking companions, also winter camping enthusiasts, planned to climb Mount Marcy over Halloween weekend 1968. My friends Jay Sulzberger and Larry Brooks would drive from Boston, Massachusetts. Our mountain mentor, Professor Jack MacIntosh, would drive from Wesleyan University in Middletown, Connecticut . I would drive from New York City with fellow Columbia student Frank Rosenthal in my 1954 Buick. We planned to meet at Heart Lake and then camp on the summit of Mount Marcy. Perhaps that was a foolish idea in any season. It certainly was a foolish idea in October.

A word about the 1954 Buick. I purchased it in Jackson, Wyoming with my climbing buddy Dave Ingalls. We drove the car back to New York the long way, through Colorado, Texas, Arkansas and Tennessee, and then up the length of the Great Smoky Mountains and Shenandoah National Parks, on the Blue Ridge Parkway and the Skyline Drive. We forgot all about the fireworks in the trunk. We had purchased them legally in Wyoming.

Frank and I left New York late on a Friday night—in plenty of time for our rendezvous Saturday morning. South of Albany, we pulled off the New York State Thruway. We napped in a field. A state trooper nudged us awake at dawn with his boot.

"You can't sleep here," he said. "Move on."

"Okay," we mumbled groggily.

"By the way," the trooper said, "Would you boys mind opening the trunk of the car?"

Not wanting to cause a ruckus, we did. We were as surprised as the trooper to find the trunk load of illegal (in New York State) fireworks.

"You're in trouble now," he said.

Coming of Age Stories

He hustled us into his squad car and not long after, we hauled up in Judge Albano's court room. I was contrite, ready to pay a fine and move on. Frank, not so much. It was the 1960s. "This is outrageous police injustice," he shouted at the judge.

The judge didn't appreciate Frank's attitude. Looking at me, he levied a fine of 25 dollars. I was able to pay that. Looking at Frank, the Judge said, "Son, how much money do you have on you?"

Frank looked in his wallet and said, "25 dollars."

"Your bail is set at 35 dollars," the Judge said. The bailiff and the trooper hustled Frank back into the squad car, destination Albany County jail.

Frank was in jail. What to do? Jay and Larry were en route from Boston. Jack MacIntosh was on his way from Middletown. This was forty years before everyone had a phone on their person. I hitchhiked from the courthouse to the first rest area on New York's Northway. I hoped I was in front of my companions as I stuck my thumb out. If not, I would catch up with them on the trail. Too bad for Frank. He languished in jail.

Jack MacIntosh came along within ten minutes, Jay and Larry five minutes later. We toddled off directly to the Albany County Jail, which still today is located very conveniently beside the Northway. We sprang Frank within an hour. While Frank's court case dragged on for months, and the car remained impounded until I snuck into the impound yard one night months later, we were all together and on the trail up Mount Marcy by lunchtime.

The wind blew so fiercely on the summit that the tent poles broke in one of our two tents. The five of us spent a freezing night in a single small tent.

That 1968 Halloween was so memorable that we resolved to repeat the experience in 1969. With a much larger party and a large, round tent capable of holding fourteen good friends, we camped in bitter conditions at Plateau, an hour below Marcy's summit. The outlines of the annual rite took shape: good friends, good food, a case of champagne, and bacchanalian rituals around the oversize pumpkin. The ceremony would move around over the years. We preferred Lake Tear of the Clouds on Marcy's north side to Plateau on Marcy's south side. In the 1980s, we relocated to the Johns Brook Valley, a longer approach to Marcy. If the weather was good, the pumpkin still made it to the top of Marcy. If it was not so good, we placed the pumpkin on Big Slide, or another more accessible summit.

Brushes with authority became a concern as the group size exceeded the Adirondack Park limit of twelve. We celebrated on the flanks of Hurricane Mountain where no one would care about us. We returned to the Johns Brook Valley. Renting space from the private Adirondack Mountain Club circumvented the group-size limitation. As we aged, our ambition tapered. In the 1990s, we held several Halloweens at a private farm in the southern Adirondacks, which was easier to get to and the barn on the property offered a refuge from the abysmal weather at that time of year. By the millennium, we had downscaled further, meeting at Chez Pierre restaurant in South Glens Falls, New York. (Chez Pierre, with its classic French menu is still going strong. I commend it to anyone in the area.)

I am fortunate to have field notes from some of the Halloween hikes. Regarding that first weekend, the notes say simply, "Tent blew out in the wind. Trip instantly recognized as a tradition." Regarding the repeat trip in 1969 with fourteen people and the circus tent, my notes record an inch of snow at Plateau lean-to with high winds. We cooked twelve pounds of steak over a bonfire. The pumpkin ceremony was inaugurated in all its gory glory.

The 1970 hike was the first to follow the Johns Brook trail. The group stayed the night at Slant rock Lean-to. The pumpkin was placed atop Little Haystack, not Mount Marcy. The weather was unseasonably warm, and quite rainy. The group returned to the Indian Falls trail (Plateau) in 1971. A two a.m. storm brought sleet and high wind.

We brought tarps and lanterns up to Lake Tear in 1972, to accommodate our growing numbers. The pumpkin weighed 84 pounds. The frozen ground melted in the rain. Everyone arrived muddy and cold. The term "sincere" was first applied to the Halloween hikers, as in, "You must be sincerely committed in order to hike this weekend." (Ambiguity intended.) Chez Pierre won our hearts by welcoming our muddied, bedraggled lot into their fine dining establishment that Sunday night. "We've been expecting you," they said delightedly.

The Year of Great Excess. (Betsy Cheney and Jack Macintosh)

We continued to hold the arcane rites at Lake Tear for at least the next five years. Because of the quantities of spirits imbibed, the amount of food packed in, and the outrageous behavior of our growing party of revelers, 1975 became known as the year of great excess. We picked up a mysterious woman, whom we called Miss Tunisia. She lost her pants in the middle of the night. From my notes, "Supplies included a case of champagne, bottles of vodka and ouzo, and "fang," a lethal combination of 151-proof rum and tang. Wolfgang jumped Miss Tunisia in the lean-to. Mac lectured Marxism to a disbelieving Vernon. Jay and Susan were preoccupied with each other, noisily. Charlie could not find his tent in the dark. Joanne did not pass out this year. Larry drank champagne to excess. Vernon turned green and became entangled in dwarf spruce."

The menu in 1976, on Giant Mountain, was particularly notable, "Fresh mussels and bouillabaisse, chili and peanuts, lamb stew." We returned to Giant Mountain for our tenth anniversary trip. Again, chef Larry Brooks produced an outstanding repast, "Homemade pate, leek soup with crème, lamb curry with homemade chutney, chestnuts, Peking duck with pancakes, chili, apple crisp."

And so it continued, year after year for three more decades. Even after I moved to Washington, D.C., I trekked to the Adirondacks for Halloween. The year 1987 was particularly memorable. My colleague Lincoln Crane had recently obtained a pilot's license and purchased a Cessna. Linc liked to hike, so I invited him on the Halloween weekend. We planned to fly his Cessna up to the Adirondacks for the overnight, then return. We left at dawn. It didn't occur to me to ask Linc about his piloting experience until we were at 7,000 feet over Harrisburg, Pennsylvania, lost in a cloud bank. We spiraled crazily down to scoot under the clouds. Linc asked me to read the highway signs below to get a bead on our location and direction.

"How long have you been flying?" I asked.

"You're my first and only non-family, non-instructor passenger!" he said.

We landed in Glens Falls, New York, rented a car and drove up to Keene Valley, then hiked four miles to the lean-to to join the rest of the crew. After the annual Halloween nighttime debauchery, Linc retraced his steps the following morning so that he could land his plane on Keene Valley's mountain-ringed grass air strip. That afternoon, as I descended Brothers Mountain, I heard Linc's Cessna buzzing overhead.

Landing was only half the fun. Taking off from the grass strip involved a full throttle run at a forest wall and then a sharp 180 degree climbing turn. The rest of the flight was memorable for the clear sky and smooth ride.

After I moved to the West Coast, I continued to attend the annual Adirondack gatherings until the old crew became too infirm to continue. Rain or shine (usually rain or sleet), there is nothing like old friends. Old hiking companions are in our thoughts and in our hearts. They continue to be my trail companions in memory even now.

Chapter 15

Coda

My explorations in my teens and twenties took me to the corners of the earth, to the frontiers of knowledge. They involved tentative friendships, some of which blossomed into lifelong relationships. I was never a great musician—or mechanic or electrician—but I persevered as I explored. I hope these tales, seemingly from a distant, less connected world, inspire others on their own life journeys.

This volume of coming of age stories is the first part of a trilogy of my life. The second volume will present a compilation of travels to unusual places and encounters with interesting people from different walks of life. The final volume, written primarily for my children, grandchildren, and perhaps even great grandchildren, will recount the history of our direct ancestors, describe my youth in 1950s and 1960s Washington, DC and New York City, and my career in and around government at local, state and national levels. I will endeavor as well to describe the people most important to me, my wives, my children, mentors and friends.

Charles A. Bookman | The World Has Changed

    I want to end this volume where it began, with a shout-out to my parents, reporters both, for whom the written word was as important as hugs and kisses. These stories might have been lost if I had not spent a lifetime making notes and writing letters to friends and family. The title of this volume, "The World Has Changed" might as easily refer to the descent from thoughtful essays and descriptive letters to communication by text in 150-word bursts as anything else.

About the Author

After sailing the seas and adventuring in Africa and South America, the author studied policy and learned engineering management by inoculation. From 1978 until 1997, he advised Congress and Cabinet Departments about economic growth and the environment through his work at the National Academy of Sciences. Relocating to Seattle, Washington, he directed Traffic Operations and Street Maintenance at the Seattle Department of Transportation. Since retiring in 2012, he continues to help build successful organizations, challenge old ideas and create communities through pro bono consulting for non-profit organizations. He holds a Master of Marine Affairs degree from the University of Rhode Island and a Bachelor of Arts degree from Columbia University. He is married with two grown sons, a stepson, and (as of this writing) five grandchildren.

Made in the USA
Middletown, DE
14 July 2024